How I Know

GOD

Answers

PRAYER

Rosalind Goforth

How I Know
GOD
Answers
PRAYER

Rosalind Goforth

WHITAKER
HOUSE

Unless otherwise indicated, all Scripture quotations are taken from the King James Version of the Holy Bible. Scripture quotations marked (RV) are taken from the Revised Version of the Holy Bible.

Certain words and phrases have been printed in boldface type for emphasis by the author. However, the content of the verses remains unchanged.

HOW I KNOW GOD ANSWERS PRAYER:
Miracles from the Mission Field of Jonathan Goforth

ISBN: 978-1-62911-003-5
eBook ISBN: 978-1-62911-027-1
Printed in the United States of America
© 2014 by Whitaker House

Whitaker House
1030 Hunt Valley Circle
New Kensington, PA 15068
www.whitakerhouse.com

Library of Congress Cataloging-in-Publication Data (Pending)

1 2 3 4 5 6 7 8 9 10 11 **W** 20 19 18 17 16 15 14

CONTENTS

FOREWORD

It seems fitting that this little book of personal testimonies to answered prayer should have a brief introductory word as to how it came to be written. Some who had read a number of these testimonies as they appeared in the pages of *The Sunday School Times* have asked the question, "How could you write about such personal and sacred incidents in your life?" I could not have written them except for a very clear, God-given leading.

The story is as follows: When my husband and I were in Canada on our first furloughs, I was frequently amazed at the incredulity people expressed when definite testimony was given regarding an answer to prayer. Sometimes this was shown by an expressive shrug of the shoulders, sometimes by a sudden silence or a turning of the topic of conversation, and sometimes more openly by the query "How do you know that it might not have happened so anyway?"

Gradually, the impression deepened. I thought to myself, *If they will not believe one, two, or a dozen testimonies, will they believe the combined testimonies of one whole life?*

The more I thought about what it would mean to record the sacred incidents of my life connected with answers to prayer, the more I shrank from the publicity and from undertaking the task. There were dozens of answers to prayer far too sacred for the public eye. Some were known only by a few people, and others were known only by God. But I knew that if the record were to carry weight with those who did not believe in the supernatural work of prayer, I would have to make public many personal and scarcely less sacred incidents.

Again and again, I laid the matter aside as impossible. But I know now that the thing was from God. As months, even years, passed, the impelling sense that the record of God's answers to my prayers *must* be written gave me no rest.

It was at the close of the 1908–10 furlough, during which, as a family, we had been blessed with many—and, to our weak faith, wonderful—answers to prayer that my oldest son urged me to record in some definite form the answers to prayer in my life, and he extracted from me a solemn promise that I would do it.

But months after we returned to China, the record had still not been touched. Then came a sudden and serious illness that threatened my life, and the doctor told me I must not delay in getting my affairs in order.

It was then that an overwhelming sense of regret took possession of me that I had not written down the prayer testimonies, and I solemnly covenanted with the Lord that if He would raise me up, I would write them down.

There was no more question of what others might think; my only thought was to obey. The Lord raised me up, and although He had to deal with me very sternly once more before I really set myself to the task, the testimonies that are given here were written at last—most of them in odd moments of time during strenuous missionary journeys among the heathen.

Thus it will be seen that these incidents of answered prayer are not presented as being more wonderful or more worthy of record than multitudes the world over could testify to, but they are written and sent out simply and only because *I had to write them or disobey God.*

—*Rosalind Goforth*

1

Getting Things from God

"Are not five sparrows sold for two farthings, and not one of them is forgotten before God?...Fear not therefore: ye are of more value than many sparrows."
—Luke 12:6–7

The pages of this little book deal almost wholly with just one aspect of prayer—petition. This record is almost entirely a personal testimony of what petition to my heavenly Father has meant to me in meeting the everyday crises of my life.

A prominent Christian worker who had read some of these testimonies in *The Sunday School Times* once said to me, "To emphasize getting things from God, as you do, is to make prayer too material."

To me, this seems far from true. God is my Father; I am His child. As truly as I delight to be sought by my child when he is cold, hungry, ill, or in need of protection, so it is with my heavenly Father.

Prayer has been hedged in with too many man-made rules. I am convinced that God intended prayer to be as simple and natural, and as constant a part of our spiritual lives, as the interaction between a child and his parent in the home. And just as a large part of the interaction between a child and his parent is simply acts of asking and receiving, so it is with us and our heavenly Parent.

Perhaps, however, the most blessed element of this asking and receiving from God is the subsequent strengthening of faith that comes when a definite request has been granted. What can be more helpful and inspiring than a ringing testimony of what God has done?

As I have recalled the past in writing these incidents, one of my most precious memories is that of an evening when a number of friends had gathered in our home. The conversation turned to the topic of answered prayer. For more than two hours, we vied with one another in recounting personal incidents of God's wonderful work, and the inspiration of that evening still abides with me today.

A Christian minister once said to me, "Is it possible that the great God of the universe, the Maker and Ruler of mankind, could or would, as you would make out, take interest in such a trifle as the trimming of a hat? To me, it is preposterous!"

Yet did not our Lord Jesus Christ say, "*The very hairs of your head are all numbered*" (Matthew 10:30); "*Not one [sparrow] is forgotten before God*" (Luke 12:6); and, "*Your Father knoweth what things ye have need of, before ye ask him*" (Matthew 6:8)?

It is true that "there is nothing too great for God's power"; and it is just as true that "there is nothing too small for His love!"

If we believe God's Word, we must believe that, as missionary Dan Crawford has succinctly and beautifully expressed it, "the God of the infinite is the God of the infinitesimal." Yes, He is the...

> God who clears the grounding berg
> And steers the grinding floe,
> He hears the cry of the little kit-fox
> And the lemming on the snow.[1]

Perhaps there has never been a more wonderful testimony of God's willingness to help in every emergency of life than that which Mary Slessor gave when she was asked to tell what prayer had meant to her. She wrote,

> My life is one long daily, hourly, record of answered prayer. For physical health, for mental overstrain, for guidance given marvellously, for errors and dangers averted, for enmity to the Gospel subdued, for food provided at the exact hour needed, for everything that goes to make up life and my poor service, I can testify with a full and often wonder-stricken awe that I believe God answers prayer. I know God answers prayer.[2]

I have been asked the question, "Has God *always* given you just what you have asked for?"

---

1. Rudyard Kipling, "The Rhyme of the Three Sealers."
2. Mary Slessor quoted in James H. Smith, *Our Faithful God: Answers to Prayer* (1898), also quoted in William Pringle Livingstone, *Mary Slessor of Calabar: Pioneer Missionary* (New York: Hodder and Stoughton, 1916), 293.

Oh, no! For Him to have done so would have been great unkindness. For instance, when I was a young woman, I prayed for three years that God would grant me a certain petition. Sometimes I pleaded for this answer as if I were pleading for life itself, so intensely did I want it. Then God showed me very clearly that I was praying against His will. I resigned my will to His in the matter, and, a few months later, God gave what was infinitely better. I have often praised Him for denying that prayer, for had He granted it, I never could have come to China.

Then, too, we must remember that many of our prayers, though always heard, are not granted because of some sin harbored in our life, or because of our unbelief, or because of our failure to meet some other biblical condition governing prevailing prayer. (See "Causes of Failure in Prayer" in chapter 9.)

The following incidents of answered prayer are by no means a complete record. How could they be, when I kept no record of prayer all these fifty years? Had I done so, I do not doubt that volumes could have been written to the glory of God's grace and power in answering prayer. But even from what is recorded here, I, too, can say from a full heart, *I know God answers prayer.*

> He answered prayer: so sweetly that I stand
> Amid the blessing of His wondrous hand
> And marvel at the miracle I see,
> The favors that His love hath wrought for me.
> Pray on for the impossible, and dare

Upon thy banner this brave motto bear,
 "My Father answers prayer."

2

Early Lessons in the Life of Faith

"I love the Lord, *because he hath heard my voice
and my supplications."*
—Psalm 116:1

When I was a very little child so young that I can remember nothing earlier, a severe thunderstorm passed over our home. Terrified, I ran to my mother, who placed my hands together and pointed upward, repeating one word over and over again: "Jesus."

More than fifty years have passed since that day, but the impression that was left upon my childish mind of a Being invisible but able to hear and help has never been erased.

My most precious recollections from early childhood are associated with the stories told to me by my mother, many of which illustrate the power of prayer.

Led by a Bird

One that made an especially deep impression on me was about my grandfather, who, as a little boy, went to visit his cousins in the south of England. Their home was situated close to a dense forest, and one day, he and his cousins, lured by the beautiful wildflowers, became hopelessly lost in the woods. After trying in vain to find a way out, the eldest child, a young girl, called the frightened, crying little ones to gather around her and said to them, "When mother died, she told us to always tell Jesus if we were in any trouble. Let us kneel down and ask Him to take us home."

They knelt, and as she prayed, one of the little ones opened his eyes and saw a bird so close to his hand that he reached out for it. The bird hopped away but kept very close to the child as to lead him on. Soon, all were joining in the chase after the bird, which flew just above them and hopped on the ground in front of them, sometimes almost within reach. Then, suddenly, it flew into the air and went away. The children looked up to find themselves on the edge of the woods and in sight of home.

With such influences bearing upon me at an impressionable age, it is not surprising that even as a very little child, I began to just "tell Jesus" when I was in trouble.

Toothache Taken Away

Through the mists of memory, I clearly recall one incident that occurred when I was six or seven years of age. One day while playing in the garden, I was seized with what we then called a "jumping" toothache. I ran to my mother for comfort, but nothing she could do seemed to ease the pain.

The nerve must have become exposed, for the pain was acute. Suddenly, I thought, *Jesus can help me*; and just as I was, with my face pressed against my mother's breast, I said in my heart, "Lord Jesus, if You will take away this toothache right now, *now*, I will be Your little girl for three years."

Before I fully finished my prayer, the pain was entirely gone. I believed that Jesus had taken it away, and the result was that for years, when tempted to be naughty, I was afraid to do what I knew was wrong, lest the toothache return because I had broken my side of what I felt was a covenant with God.

This little incident had a big influence on my early life; it gave me a constant sense of the reality of a divine presence and therefore helped to prepare me for my public confession of Christ as my Savior a few years later, at the age of eleven.

Reward of Seeking First the Kingdom

About a year after my confession of Christ, an incident occurred that greatly strengthened my faith and led me to look to God as a Father in a new way.

On Easter Sunday morning, it was so warm outside that lightweight spring clothes were called for. However, my sister decided at breakfast that we would not go to church, since we had only our old winter dresses to wear. Going to my room, I turned to my Bible to study it, when it opened to the sixth chapter of Matthew. My eyes rested on these words: *"Why take ye thought for raiment?…Seek ye first the kingdom of God, and his righteousness; and all these things shall be added unto you"* (Matthew 6:28, 33). It was as if God spoke the words directly to me. I determined to go to church, even if I had to humiliate myself by going in my old winter dress. The Lord was true to His promise; I can still feel the power that the resurrection messages had upon my heart that day so long ago. Furthermore, on the following day, a box arrived from a distant aunt, containing not only new dresses but many other things that might well be included in the *"all these things."*

Financial Aid

An unforgettable proof of God's loving care came to us as a family about this time, when my parents were face-to-face with a serious financial crisis. We depended on a quarterly income, which came through my mother's lawyer in England. Unusual circumstances had so drained our resources that we found ourselves, in the middle of the quarter, with funds barely sufficient to meet a week's needs. My dear mother assured us that the Lord would provide and that He would not forsake those who put their trust in Him. That very day, a letter came from the lawyer in England, enclosing a draft for a sum ample to meet our needs until the regular remittance should arrive. This unexpected and timely draft proved to be a divine blessing, for it did not occur again. Isaiah 65:24 had been literally fulfilled: *"Before they call, I will answer; and while they are yet speaking, I will hear."*

Given Pupils for Sunday School

Some years later, having moved to a strange city, great longing came to me to do some definite service for my Master. One day in Bible class, I was informed of a need for teachers to aid in a Sunday school nearby. When I presented myself before the superintendent of that school the following week-end, offering my services, it is not much wonder I received a rebuff, for I was young and quite unknown. I was told that if

I wished to teach a class, it would be well for me to find my own pupils. I can remember how a lump in my throat seemed to be choking me all the way home that day.

At last, determining not to be baffled, I prayed to the Lord to help me get some scholars. I went forth, praying every step of the way. The following Saturday afternoon, I canvassed children who lived near our home and received the promise of nineteen children to attend Sunday school. The next day, feeling a rather victorious young woman, I walked up to the Sunday school superintendent with seventeen children following. Needless to say, I was given a class.

Guidance in Time of Crisis

In the autumn of 1885, the Toronto Mission Union, a faith mission, decided to establish a branch mission in the East End slums of that city. I and three others were deputed to open this work. Everything connected with it was entirely new to me, but I found it most helpful and inspiring, for in the face of tremendous difficulties, which seemed to my inexperienced eyes insurmountable, I learned that prayer was the secret that overcame every obstacle, the key that unlocked every closed door.

I felt like a child learning a new and wonderful lesson as I saw benches, tables, chairs, a stove, fuel, lamps, oil, and even an organ come in answer to definite prayer for these things. But the best sight of all was when men and women, deep in sin, were converted and changed into workers for God, in answer to prayer. Praise God for the lessons then learned, which were invaluable later on when facing the heathens.

The time came when two diverse paths lay before me—
one to go to England as an artist; the other to go to China as
a missionary. My circumstances made making a definite decision most difficult. I thought I had tried every means to find
out God's will for me, and no light had come.

But in a day of great trouble, when my precious mother's
very life seemed to hang in the balance, I shut myself up with
God's Word, praying earnestly for Him to guide me to some
passage by which I might know His will for my life. I opened
my Bible to John chapter 15, and verse 16 seemed to come as
a message to me, *"Ye have not chosen me, but I have chosen you,
and ordained you, that ye should go and bring forth fruit"* (John
15:16). When I went to my dear mother and told her of the
message God had given me, she said, "I dare not fight against
God."

From that time, the last hindrance from going to China
was removed. Surely the wonderful way God has kept His
child in China for more than thirty years is proof that this
"call" was not a mistaken one. *"In all thy ways acknowledge
him, and he will direct thy paths"* (Proverbs 3:6 RV).

A Beautiful Seal on the New Life

During the summer of 1887, a book written by Dr.
Hudson Taylor came into my hands. In *China's Spiritual Needs
and Claims*, Taylor told many instances of God's gracious
provision in answer to prayer, and they impressed me deeply.
A little later, a few weeks before I was married, I found that I
was fifty dollars short of what I would need to be married free
of debt; so I resolved not to let others know of my need but to
trust God to send the money to me. The thought came, *If you*

cannot trust God for this, when Hudson Taylor could trust for so much more, are you worthy to be a missionary?

It was my first experience of trusting for money without telling anyone. I was sorely tempted to hint others of my need. But I was kept back from doing so, and though I had a week or more of severe testing, peace of mind and the assurance that God would supply my need came at length. The answer, however, did not come until the night before the wedding.

That evening, a number of my fellow workers from the East End Mission visited, and they presented me with a beautifully illuminated address and purse. After these friends had left, I returned to my family members, who were assembled in the back parlor, and showed them the address and the purse. Not for a moment had I thought that there was anything in the purse until my brother said, "You foolish girl, why don't you open it?" I opened the purse and found that it contained a check for fifty dollars!

This incident has ever remained particularly precious, for it seemed to us a seal of God upon the new life opening before us.

3

GO FORWARD ON YOUR KNEES
1887–1894

"I will go before thee, and make the crooked places straight:
I will break in pieces the gates of brass,
and cut in sunder the bars of iron."
—Isaiah 45:2

I n attempting to record what prayer meant in to our little band of missionaries in our early pioneer days, I must give more than purely personal testimonies; for we were closely knit together in our common needs and dangers.

In October 1887, my husband was appointed by the Canadian Presbyterian Church to open a new field in the northern section of the Province of Honan, China. We left Canada the following January and reached China in March 1888. Not till then did we realize the tremendous difficulties of the task before us.

Dr. Hudson Taylor, founder of the China Inland Mission, wrote to us at this time and said, "We understand North

Honan is to be your field; we, as a mission, have tried for ten years to enter that province from the south, and have only just succeeded. It is one of the most anti-foreign provinces in China...Brother, if you would enter that province, you must go forward on your knees."

These words were the keynote to our early pioneer years. Would that a faithful record had been kept of God's faithfulness in answering prayer. During those years so fraught with dangers and difficulties, our strength as both a mission and as individuals lay in the fact that we realized the hopelessness of our task apart from divine aid.

Help in Language from the Home Base

The following incident occurred while we were still outside Honan, studying the language at a sister mission. It illustrates the importance of prayer from the home base for those on the field.

My husband was having great difficulty in acquiring the language; he faithfully studied many hours daily but made painfully slow progress. Together, he and his colleague went regularly to the street chapel to practice preaching to the people in Chinese; but, though Mr. Goforth had come to China almost a year before the other missionary, the people would ask the latter to speak instead of Mr. Goforth, saying they understood him better.

One day, just before leaving for the chapel, my husband said, "If the Lord does not give me very special help in this language, I fear I will be a failure as a missionary."

Several hours later, he returned, his face beaming with joy. He told me that he had received the most unusual help when his turn came to speak. Sentences had come to his mind as never before, and not only had he expressed himself clearly, but some of the listeners had appeared much moved, coming up afterward to have further conversation with him. So delighted and encouraged with this experience was he that he made a careful note of it in his diary.

Around two and a half months later, a letter came from a student at Knox College, saying that a number of students had met on a certain evening to pray for Mr. Goforth. The power of prayer and the presence of God were so manifestly felt that they decided to write and ask Mr. Goforth if any special help had come to him at the time of their prayer. Looking in his diary, he found that the time of their meeting matched with that time he had been given special help in the language.

I cannot tell why there should come to me
A thought of someone miles and years away,
In swift insistence on the memory,
Unless there is a need that I should pray.

We are too busy to spare thought
For days together of some friends away;
Perhaps God does it for us—and we ought
To read His signal as a sign to pray.

Perhaps just then my friend has fiercer fight,
A more appalling weakness, a decay
Of courage, darkness, some lost sense of right
And so, in case he needs my prayers—I pray.

Deliverance in the Time of Peril

At last, the joyful news that our brethren had secured property in two centers reached us women as we waited outside of Honan. It would be difficult for those in the homeland to understand what the years of waiting had meant to some of us. The danger facing those dear to us, who were touring in Honan, was very great. For years, they never left us to go on tour without our being filled with dread, lest they should never return. Yet the Lord, in His mercy, heard our prayers for them, and though they were often in grave danger, none received serious injury. This is not a history of the mission, but I cannot forbear sharing here one incident illustrating how they were kept during those early days.

After renting property in a town just within the border of Honan, near the Wei River, two of our brethren decided to move in, intending to spend the winter there. But a sudden and bitter persecution arose just as they settled down. The mission premises were attacked by a mob, and everything was looted. The two men were roughly handled, one having been dragged around the courtyard. At last, they found themselves alone, their lives spared, but everything gone.

Their situation was extremely serious—they were a several days' journey away from friends; they had no money, no bedding, and no clothes but those they were wearing; and the cold winter had just begun.

In their need, they knelt down and committed themselves to the Lord. And, according to His promise, He delivered them out of their distresses, for even while they prayed, a brother missionary from a distant station was at hand. He arrived unexpectedly, only a few hours after the looting had taken place, without knowing what had occurred. His coming at such an opportune moment filled the hearts of their heathen enemies with fear. Money and goods were returned, and from that time on, the violent opposition of the natives toward the missionaries ceased.

A few months after the incident, several families moved into Honan, and a permanent occupation was established there; but the hearts of the people seemed as opposed to us as they had been before. They hated and distrusted us as if we were their worst enemies. The district in which we settled was known for its turbulent and antiforeign spirit; and as a band of missionaries, we were frequently in the gravest danger.

Many times, we realized that we, as well as our fellow workers at the other stations, were kept from serious harm by only the overruling, protecting power of God in answer to the many prayers that were going up for us all at this critical juncture in the history of our mission. The following are concrete examples of how God heard and answered our prayers.

Prayer and Medical Work[3]

We had a man of splendid gifts as our station doctor. He was a gold medalist, had years of special training and hospital experience, and was looked upon as one of the rising physicians in the city from which he came. Imagine his disappointment, therefore, when month after month passed and scarcely a good case came to the hospital. The people did not

---

3. In all the cases of divine healing cited in this book, it should be noted that God healed in answer to our prayers when the doctors had done all they could do and hope had been abandoned, or when we were out of reach of medical aid.

know what he could do; moreover, they were afraid to entrust themselves into his hands. Our little band of missionaries began to pray that the Lord would send cases to the hospital that would open the hearts of the people toward us and our message.

It was not long before we saw this prayer answered beyond all expectation. Several very important cases came almost at the same time, one so serious that the doctor hesitated for days before operating. At last, when the operation did take place, the doctor's hands were strengthened by our prayers. The patient came through safely and, only a few days later, he went around town and was a living wonder to the people.

Much depended upon the outcome of this and other serious operations. Had the patients died at the doctor's hands, it would have been quite sufficient to cause the destruction of the mission and the life of every missionary.

Three years later, the hospital records showed that there had been twenty-eight thousand treatments in one year.

Again, we kept praying that the Lord would give us converts. We had heard of missionaries in India, China, and elsewhere who had worked for many years without gaining converts, but we did not believe that this was God's will for us. We believed that it was His pleasure and purpose to save men and women through His human channels, and so, we thought, *Why wouldn't He do it from the beginning?* We kept praying and working and expecting converts, and God gave them to us. Our experience of thirty years has confirmed this belief.

Early Converts

The first convert was Wang Feng-ao, who came with us to Honan as Mr. Goforth's personal teacher. He was a man of high degree, equal to the Western M.A., and was one of the proudest and most overbearing Confucian scholars I'd ever met. He despised the missionaries and their teaching, and so great was his opposition that he would beat his wife every time she came to see us or listen to our message. But Mr. Goforth kept praying for this man and using all his influence to win him for Christ.

Before long, a great change came over Mr. Wang. His proud, overbearing manner had changed, and he became a humble, devout follower of the lowly Nazarene. God had used a dream to awaken this man's conscience, which is not uncommon in China. One night, he'd dreamt he was struggling in a deep, miry pit, but as much as he'd tried, he had not been able to find a way of escape. About to give up in despair, he'd looked up and seen Mr. Goforth and another missionary on the bank above him, with their hands stretched out to save him. Again, he'd sought for some other way of escape, but finding none, he'd allowed them to draw him up.

Later on, this man became Mr. Goforth's most valued evangelist. For many years, his splendid gifts were used to the glory of his Master in his work among the scholar class in the Changtefu district. He has long since passed on to receive his reward, dying as he had lived, trusting only in the merit of Jesus Christ for salvation.

Another bright light in the darkness of those early days in Honan was the remarkable conversion of Wang Fu-Lin.

For many years, his business had been that of a public storyteller, but when Mr. Goforth came across him, Fu-Lin was reduced to an utter wreck because of opium smoking. He accepted the gospel, but for a long time, he seemed too weak to break the opium habit. Again and again, he tried to do so, but failed miserably each time.

The poor fellow seemed almost past hope, when one day, Mr. Goforth brought him to the mission in his cart. The ten days that followed can never be forgotten by those who watched Wang Fu-Lin struggle for his physical and spiritual life. I truly believe that nothing but prayer could have brought him through. At the end of the ten days, the power of opium was broken, and Wang Fu-Lin emerged from the struggle a new man in Christ Jesus. I will have occasion to speak of this man again.

Rev. Hunter Corbett's Testimony

Soon after coming to China, the Rev. Hunter Corbett, one of the most devoted and saintly of God's missionaries, gave a testimony that later was used by God to save me from giving up my term of service in China and returning home to Canada.

Dr. Corbett said that for fifteen years, he had been laid aside every year with that terrible scourge of the East—dysentery; and the doctors at last told him that he must return at once to the homeland and forsake China. But the grand old man said, "I knew God had called me to China, and I also knew that God did not change. So what could I do? I dared not go back on my call. So I determined that if I could not live in China, I could die there, and from that time on, the disease lost its hold on me."

This testimony was given over twenty-five years ago, when he had already been in China for almost thirty years! In January 1920, when approaching ninety years of age, this beloved and honored saint of God passed on to higher service.

For several years, I was affected with dysentery just as Dr. Corbett had been, and each year, the terrible disease seemed to get a firmer hold upon me. At last, my husband informed me of the decision of the doctors that I should return home. And as I lay there ill and weak, the temptation came to yield. But, as I remembered Dr. Corbett's testimony and my own clear call, I felt that to go back would be to go against my own conscience. I therefore determined to do as Dr. Corbett had done—leave myself in the Lord's hands—whether for life or for death. This happened more than twenty years ago, and since then, I have had very little trouble from that dreadful disease.

Yes, the deeper the need and the more bitter the extremity, the greater the opportunity for God to show forth His mighty power in our lives, if we but give Him a chance by steadily obeying Him at any cost. *"In the day when I cried thou answeredst me, and strengthenedst me with strength in my soul"* (Psalm 138:3).

A Test of Obedience

During our fourth year in China, when we were spending the hot season at the coast, our little son, only eighteen months old at the time, was taken very ill with dysentery. After the child's several days' fight for life, I realized one evening that the angel of death was at hand.

My whole soul rebelled. I actually seemed to hate God. I could see nothing but cruel injustice in it all, and the child seemed to be going fast. My husband and I knelt down beside the little one's bed, and he pleaded earnestly with me to yield my will and my child to God. After a long and bitter struggle, God gained the victory, and I told my husband that I would give my child to the Lord. Then my husband prayed, committing the precious soul into the Lord's keeping.

While he was praying, I noticed that the rapid, hard breathing of the child had ceased. Thinking my darling was gone, I hastened for a light, for it was dark, but on examining the child's face, I found that he had sunk into a deep, sound, natural sleep, which lasted most of the night. The following day, he was practically well of dysentery.

To me, it has always seemed that the Lord tests me to my limit. Then, when I yield my dearest treasure to Him and put Him first, He gives back the child.

I just came across an excerpt from *The Christian* published on March 12, 1914, in which the editor said:

Speaking at the annual meeting of the Huntingdon County Hospital, Lord Sandwich referred to the power of spiritual healing, and premising that the finite mind cannot measure the power of the infinite, said he "looked forward to the day when the spiritual doctrine of healing and the physical discoveries of science will blend in harmonious combination, to the glory of God and the benefit of humanity."

4

A God-Given Field
1894–1900

*"Lord, there is none beside thee to help, between the mighty
and him that hath no strength: help us, O Lord our God;
for we rely on thee, and in thy name are we come
against this multitude."*
—2 Chronicles 14:11 (rv)

The story of the opening of Changte is so connected by a
chain of prayer that to give isolated instances of intercession would be to break the chain.

A few months after our arrival in China, an old, experi-
enced missionary kindly volunteered to conduct Mr. Goforth
and his colleague, who had just arrived, through North
Honan, so that they might see the field for themselves.

Traveling southward by cart, they crossed the border into
Honan early one morning. As my husband walked beside the
carts, he felt led to pray that the Lord would give that section
of Honan to him as a field for harvesting. And the assurance

came that his prayer was granted. Opening his daily text-
book, he found that the passage for that morning was from
Isaiah 55:8–13. The words were like a precious promise of
future blessing:

> *As the rain cometh down, and the snow from heaven,*
> *and returneth not thither, but watereth the earth, and*
> *maketh it bring forth and bud, that it may give seed to*
> *the sower, and bread to the eater: so shall my word be*
> *that goeth forth out of my mouth: it shall not return*
> *unto me void.* (Isaiah 55:10–11)

For six years, however, our faith was sorely tested.

Of all the places we went, the people of Changte seemed
the most determined to keep out the missionaries. And there
were other difficulties in the way. A presbytery had been
formed as others joined us, and all matters had to be decided
by that body. Two stations that had been opened where a
foothold could first be gained required all, and sometimes
more than all, the force we then had. So for six years, the
door to Changte remained closed, but during all those years,
Mr. Goforth never once lost sight of God's promise to him or
failed to believe it.

Again and again, when Mr. Goforth and his colleague
visited the city, they were mobbed and threatened, the
people showing them utmost hostility. But the day came, at
last, when the long-prayed-for permission from the presbytery to open Changte was granted. The very next morning,
Mr. Goforth was en route for Changte to secure property
for a mission site. Often he has told how, on his way over to
Changte that day, he had prayed for the Lord to open the

hearts of the people and to make them willing to give him the property most suitable for the work. Within three days of his reaching Changte, he had thirty-five offers of property and was able to secure the very piece of land he had chosen earlier as the most ideal location for the mission. Thus the Lord broke into pieces the gates of brass that had kept us so long from our promised land.

A year later, I joined my husband there with our three little children. It was arranged that our colleague would take charge of the outside evangelism, while we opened work at the main station.

Our Great Need

To understand what it meant for us to have our need supplied, there must be some knowledge of what that need was.

We decided, from the onset, that no one should be turned away from our doors. So Mr. Goforth received all men in the front guest room, while the women and children came to our private quarters. During those first weeks and months, hundreds—no, thousands—came to see us. Day by day, we were besieged. Even at mealtime, our windows were banked with faces.

The questions ever before us those days were how to make the most of this wonderful opportunity, which would never come again after the period of curiosity was past; how to win the friendship of this people, who showed their hatred and distrust of us in a hundred ways; and how to reach their hearts with the wonderful message of a Savior's love.

Day by day, all that was in our power was to do what we could with the strength that was given us. From early morning till dark, and sometimes nine or ten hours a day, we felt the strain of receiving and preaching to these crowds. My husband had to oversee numbers of workmen and organize and execute the one-hundred-and-one things that were necessary in building up a new station, such as purchasing building material. Besides all this, he had to receive, and preach to, the crowds that came.

He had no fellow evangelists aside from Mr. Wang, who was then lent to Mr. MacG—. I had my three little children and no nurse or Bible woman to help with the care. When I was too exhausted to speak any longer to the courtyard of women, I would send for my husband, who, though he was tired, would speak in my stead. Then we would rest ourselves and entertain the crowd by singing a hymn.

So the days passed. But soon we realized that help must come, or we would both break down.

One day, Mr. Goforth came to me with his Bible opened to the promise *"My God shall supply all your need"* (Philippians 4:19) and asked me, "Do we believe this? If we do, then God can and will supply us with someone to help preach to these crowds, if we ask in faith."

He prayed very definitely for a man to preach. With my doubt-blinded heart, I thought it was as if he were asking for rain from a clear sky. Yet even while he prayed, God was moving someone to come to us. A day or two later, there appeared at the mission the converted opium fiend Wang Fu-Lin.

No one could have looked less like the answer to our prayers than he did. He was fearfully emaciated from long years of excessive opium smoking, racked with a cough that ended his life three years later, and dressed in filthy rags that only a beggar would wear—he was a pitiable sight. Yet the Lord does not see as man sees.

After consulting Wang Fu-Lin, Mr. Goforth decided to try him for a few days, believing that he could at least testify to the power of God that saved him from his opium addiction. Soon, he was clothed in some of my husband's Chinese garments, and within an hour or two of his entering the mission gate, practically a beggar, he was put in charge of the men's chapel, so changed was he that one could scarcely have recognized him.

From the first day of his ministry in Changte, there was no doubt in the minds of any who heard him that he had indeed been sent to us by our gracious God, for he had, in a remarkable degree, the unction and power of the Holy Spirit. His gifts as a speaker were all consecrated to one overall goal—to win souls for Jesus Christ. He seemed conscious that his days were few, and he always spoke as a dying man to dying men. Little wonder is it, therefore, that from the very beginning of his ministry in our chapel, he won men for Christ. God spared him to help us lay the foundation of the church in Changte, then called him higher.

A Second Need Met

Mr. Goforth's need was relieved by the coming of Wang Fu-Lin, but not mine. The remarkable way God had sent him, however, gave me courage and faith to trust God to provide me with a Bible woman. Those who know anything of mission work in China will agree with me that it is far more difficult to find women who are able to preach the gospel than men; and, if able, it is even more difficult to find ones who are free for the work. But I was beginning to learn that God is limited only from the human perspective, and that He is always willing to give beyond our asking, if the conditions He has so plainly laid out in His Word are fulfilled.

A short time after I had begun to definitely ask my heavenly Father for a Bible woman, Mr. MacG— came in from a tour, and his first words to me were: "Well, Mrs. Goforth, I believe we have a ready-made Bible woman for you!"

Then he told me how he had come across a widow and her son in a mountain village, who had heard the gospel from a recent convert out of one of the other stations. This convert had been a member of the same religious sect as the widow and her son. When he found Christ, he at once thought of his friends and went over to the mountain to tell them. Mrs. Chang received the gospel gladly. She had been a preacher in that heathen sect, and had gained fluency in speaking, and power to hold the attention of audiences, which is so necessary in the preaching of the gospel.

The way was soon opened for her to come to me, and she became my constant companion and valuable assistant in the work with the women during those early years. She witnessed a good confession in 1900—being strung up by her thumbs when refusing to deny her Lord. Faithfully she served the Lord as a Bible woman, until the time of her death in 1903.

Paying the Price of Petition

During the first two or three years in Chang Te Fu, we lived in unhealthful Chinese houses, which were low and damp. It was therefore thought best that we should have a good semiforeign house built for us. The work at this time was so encouraging—converts being added weekly, and sometimes almost daily—that we feared the new house would hinder the work and become a separating barrier between us and the people. We therefore prayed that God would make the new house a means of reaching the people—a blessing, and not a hindrance. The answer to this prayer, as is often the case, depended largely upon us. We had to be made willing to pay the price.

In other words, we came to see that in order for our prayer to be answered, we would have to keep our house open every day and all day, which was by no means easy. Some people assured us it was wrong, because it would make us cheap in the eyes of the Chinese; others said it was wrong because it made our children susceptible to infection. But time proved these objections unfounded. The very highest as well as the lowest were received, and their friendship won by this means. And, insofar as I can remember, our children never caught any contagion from this way of receiving the people into our house.

The climax in numbers was reached in the spring of 1899, when we received 835 men and several hundred women in one day. First, we preached to them in large bands, and then we led them through the house. We have seen evidences of the good of this plan in all parts of our field. It opened the hearts of the people toward us, and it helped us to live down suspicion and distrust as nothing else could have done.

A Touch of Healing

In May of 1898, Mr. Goforth and I started down to Tientsin by houseboat with our children for a much-needed rest and change. Cold, wet weather soon set in. Twelve days later, as we came in sight of Tientsin, with a bitter north wind blowing, our eldest child went out on deck without his overcoat, disobeying my orders. Then he came in with a violent chill, and that afternoon, when we arrived in Tientsin, the doctors pronounced the verdict—pneumonia.

Shortly after noon the following day, a second doctor who had been consulted met a friend on his way from our boy's bedside and told her he did not think the child would live till morning. I had taken his temperature and found it to be 106. He was extremely restless, tossing in the burning fever. Sitting down beside him, with a cry to the Lord to help me, I said, "P—, you disobeyed me, and have thus brought this illness upon yourself. I forgive you. Ask Jesus to forgive you, and give yourself to Him."

The child looked steadily at me for a moment, then closed his eyes. I saw his lips move for a moment, then he quietly sank into a sound sleep. When he awoke, about dusk, I took his temperature and found it to be 101. By the time the doctor returned, it was normal, and it did not rise again. Although he had been hemorrhaging from his lungs, this ceased, too.

Is not Jesus Christ the same yesterday, today, and forever? (See Hebrews 13:8.) Why should we wonder, then, at His healing touch in this age? *"According to your faith be it unto you"* (Matthew 9:29).

During those early pioneer years, when laying the foundation of the Changte Church, my own weak faith was often rebuked when I saw the results of the simple, childlike faith of our Chinese Christians. Some of those answers to prayer were of such an extraordinary character that, when told in the homeland, even ministers expressed doubts as to their genuineness. But, praise God, I know they are true. Here are two concrete examples.

A Chinaman's Faith

Li-ming, a warm-hearted, earnest evangelist, owned land some miles north of Chang Te Fu. On one occasion, when visiting the place, he found the neighbors all busy, placing little sticks with tiny flags around their fields. They believed this would keep the locusts from eating their grain. All of them urged Li-ming to do the same, and to worship the locust god, or, they warned, his grain would be destroyed. Li-ming replied, "I worship the one only true God, and I will pray Him to keep my grain, that you may know that He alone is God."

The locusts came and ate on all sides of Li-ming's grain but did not touch his own. When Mr. Goforth heard this story, he determined to get further proof, so he visited the place for himself and inquired of Li-ming's heathen neighbors and what they knew of the matter. One and all testified that, when the locusts had come, they had eaten their grain but not Li-ming's.

After a conflict of unbelief and hypocrisy, the Lord Jesus once said, *"I thank thee, O Father, Lord of heaven and earth, because thou hast hid these things from the wise and prudent, and hast revealed them unto babes"* (Matthew 11:25).

A Christian Woman's Faith for Her Child

Our little Grace became ill with the terribly fatal disease so common in malarious districts—an enlarged spleen. The doctors pronounced her condition quite hopeless. One day, a Chinese Christian woman came to our home with her little child who was about the same age as our Gracie and very ill with the same disease. The poor mother was in great distress, for the doctor had also told her also that there was no hope. She thought that if we would plead with the doctor, he would save her child. At last, Mr. Goforth pointed to our little Gracie, saying, "Surely, if the doctor cannot save our child, neither can he save yours; our only hope is in the Lord Himself."

The mother was a poor, hard-working, ignorant woman, but she had the simple faith of a little child. Some few weeks later, she called again and told me the following story:

When the pastor told me my only hope was in the Lord, I believed him. When I reached home, I called my husband, and together we committed our child into the Lord's hands. I felt perfectly sure the child would get well, so I did not take care of him more than I would have taken care of a well child. In about two weeks, he seemed so perfectly well that I took him to the doctor again, and the doctor said that he could discover nothing the matter with him.

A Case of Unanswered Prayer

That Chinese child is now a grown-up, healthy man. But *our child died*. We had prayed for her as few, perhaps, have prayed for any child. Why, then, had she not been spared? I do not know. But I do know that there was in my life, at that time, the sin of bitterness toward another, and an unwillingness to forgive a wrong. This was quite sufficient to hinder any prayer, and it did hinder my prayers for years, until I was set right.

Does this case of unanswered prayer shake my faith in God's willingness and power to answer prayer? No, no! My own child might just as reasonably decide never again to come to me with a request because I have, in my superior wisdom, denied a petition. Is it not true, in our relationships with our children, that we see best to grant at one time what we withhold at another? *"What I do thou knowest not now; but thou shalt know hereafter"* (John 13:7).

And one of the most precious experiences of God's loving mercy came to me in connection with our little Gracie's death. We had been warned that the end would probably come in convulsions; two of our dear children had been so taken. Only a mother who has gone through such an experience can fully understand the horror of the possibility that such a death might come again at any time.

One evening, when Miss P— and I were watching Gracie, the child said very decidedly, "Call Papa. I want to see Papa." I hesitated to awaken her father, as it was his time to rest, so I tried to put her off with some excuse; but again she repeated her request, and so I called her father, asking him to walk up and down with her until I returned.

Going into the next room, I cried out in agony to the Lord not to let Grace suffer, but, if it was indeed His will to take the child, then to do so without her suffering. As I prayed, a wonderful peace came over me, and the promise came so clearly it was as if it was spoken: *"Before they call, I will answer; and while they are yet speaking, I will hear"* (Isaiah 65:24). Rising, I was met at the door by Miss P— who said, "Gracie is with Jesus." While I was on my knees in the other room, our beloved child, after resting a few moments in her father's arms, had looked into his face with one of her loveliest smiles, then had quietly closed her eyes and ceased to breathe. No struggle, no pain, but a "falling on sleep."

> *Like as a father pitieth his children, so the* Lord *pitieth them that fear him.* (Psalm 103:13)

"A God of Deliverances"

Ever-darkening clouds gathered around us during the months following Grace's death, and while the storm did not burst in all its fury till the early summer of 1900, the preceding winter was full of forebodings and constant alarms.

On one occasion, thousands gathered inside and outside our mission, evidently bent on causing serious mischief. All that day, my husband and his colleagues moved in and out among the dense crowd that filled the front courtyards while we women remained shut within our houses, not knowing the moment the mob would break loose and destroy us all. What kept them back that day? What but trustful prayer!

The Lord heard us and wonderfully restrained the violence of our enemies.

We did not know it then, but those experiences were preparing us for the greater trials and perils awaiting us all.

5

DELIVERANCE FROM THE BOXERS
1900

"God is unto us a God of deliverances."
—Psalm 68:20 (RV)

*"Who delivered us out of so great a death, and will deliver: on
whom we have set our hope that he will also still deliver us."*
—2 Corinthians 1:10 (RV)

Many times we were asked in the homeland to tell the
story of our escape during the Boxer uprising, and
the question was often put, "If it was really God's power that
saved you and others on that journey, then why did He not
save those of His children who were so cruelly killed?"

For a time, this question troubled me. Why indeed?
One day, when seeking light on the matter, I was directed to
Acts chapter 12. There I found the only answer that can be
given. We are told in the second verse that James was put to
death by the sword; then the rest of the chapter is given to the

detailed record of Peter's wonderful deliverance in answer to prayer. (See Acts 12:2, 5, 12.)

On that day when all things will be revealed, I am convinced we will see that *prayer* had much to do in the working out of our deliverance. We were told that when our home church in Canada received the first cable informing them of our party starting on that perilous journey, a great wave of prayer went up for us from Christians of all denominations. The Presbyterian Assembly of Canada was meeting at the time, and one of their sessions was given entirely to prayer on behalf of the missionaries in China. Never had that body witnessed such a season of intense, united intercession.

Later, after giving the story of our escape in the homeland, repeatedly we have had people come up to us, telling us how, during the weeks that elapsed between the first cable informing the home church of our danger, and the second cable that told of our safe arrival at the coast, they had never ceased to cry out to God to save us.

Then, too, after all is said, we must believe that God was glorified and that His purposes were fulfilled in the death of some as in the saved lives of others. The blood of the martyrs is still the seed of the church.

Led On Through Dangers and Trials

In the month of June 1895, an incident occurred that has ever been linked in my mind with the events of 1900. I was about to leave Toronto with my four children to join my husband in China, when a cable was received telling of the cruel massacre of Mr. and Mrs. Stewart and others. Deep and widespread sympathy was expressed and much anxiety felt for missionaries, particularly those in China. Many urged me to delay our return, but I felt it best to keep to our original plans, and a few days later, we bid farewell to our friends at Union Station in Toronto.

Just as the train was leaving, a lady quickly stepped forward to the window and said, "You do not know me, but I have prayed to the Lord to give me a promise for you." She handed me a slip of paper. "It is this. Take it as from Him." I opened it and read, "*No weapon that is formed against thee shall prosper*' (Isaiah 54:17)." Then and there, I raised my heart to God in prayer that He would fulfill this promise to me and those dear to me, and as I prayed, there came the clear assurance that the Lord heard.

Never can we forget that winter of 1899–1900. The clouds had begun to gather, and we heard the rumbles of the coming storm on all sides of us. Repeatedly, our mission was in grave danger, and at such times, we were "shut up to God." The temper of the people was such that any little thing angering them would have been as a spark to gunpowder.

From the time of the government crisis of the autumn of 1899, we realized, in company with all other foreigners in China, that conditions were becoming serious, yet never did we expect or prepare for such a cataclysm as that which took place when the storm clouds suddenly burst in the early summer of 1900.

The first indication we had of coming danger was when our mail carriers, running to and from Tientsin, were stopped, and our mail was returned. Thus, cut off from the outside world, we had to depend solely upon the wild rumors circulating among the Chinese for information. The country around us became more and more disturbed; and day by day, we could hear the beating of drums and the cries of the people for rain. The darkness and horror of those days, in the midst of which sickness and death entered our home, can never be forgotten. On the nineteenth of June, our eldest daughter, Florence, after a week of intense suffering, was released from pain. It was while her life was still hanging in the balance that we received the first communication from the American consul in Chefoo urging us to flee. This message was quickly followed by another still more urgent.

The question was, where could we flee? Our usual route was by riverboat two weeks to Tientsin, but this way was blocked, the whole region being infested with Boxers, and Tientsin even then in a state of siege. The only possible route left open to us was southward by cart—a fourteen-day trip to Fancheng, and then ten or more days by houseboat to Hankow. We faced the journey that time of year with fear and trembling because of the danger the harsh heat and sun posed to the children. We would have gladly stayed, but the Chinese Christians urged us to go, saying they could escape more easily were we not there.

We had with us our four remaining children: Paul, who was nine years old; Helen, six; Ruth, under three; and baby Wallace, eight months. Their faithful Chinese nurse, though weeping bitterly at having to part from her old mother of almost eighty years, decided to come with us. Altogether, there were five men, six women, and five children in the party, besides the servants and carters.

Many were the difficulties in the way of getting carts and other necessary supplies for the journey, but one by one, all the things we needed were provided as we entreated the Lord to open the way. There were many indications on that journey that God's will was to save us; one of the most striking of these instances happened just as we were about to leave.

Safely Brought Through

The day before our departure, a message passed through the city of Chang Te Ho, and the messenger rode at breakneck speed to deliver it. This messenger, we learned later, was en route for the provincial capital with a sealed message from Empress Dowager commanding the death of all foreigners. We had first planned to take the direct route south, which, as far as we can see now, would have led us to our death, for it would have taken us through the capital. Almost at the last moment, and quite unaware of the danger on the direct route, we were led to change our plans and to take a route that was farther west, though it made a considerably longer journey.

We left Chang Te at daybreak on June 28, 1900. At Wei Hwei Fu, the first large city to which we came, an attempt was made to break into our inn, but as we prayed, the mob dispersed, and we were left in peace. On July 1, we reached the north bank of the Yellow River, and for a short time (it was Sunday afternoon), we rested there under the trees. Little did we dream that even then, many, very many, of our fellow missionaries and friends were being put to death by the merciless Boxers. At sunset, the ferry that carried us across the river reached the south bank, and here we found several missionaries and a party of engineers waiting for us. The latter were fully armed and had a fair escort. After some difficulty, it was decided that we should all stay together, but this party kept by themselves, except for staying in the same towns with us at night. Each day that passed seemed harder than the last. The heat was intense, and the ten or twelve hours of bumping over rough roads in springless carts made even a bed spread on the ground a welcome resting place.

Once, when Mr. Goforth jumped off our cart to get fresh water for our head cloths, a very threatening crowd gathered around him and cried, "Kill, kill!" All the other carts were ahead, and the driver, who was very afraid, would not wait long for Mr. Goforth. During the few moments that elapsed before my husband was allowed to rejoin us, even the carter turned pale with suspense—and oh, how I prayed!

Except for a few similar episodes, nothing special occurred until the evening of July 7, when we reached the small town of Hsintien. We had heard during the day that the country ahead of us was in a state of ferment against the Roman Catholics. We had scarcely reached the inn when the engineers and the missionaries, who had become increasingly alarmed at the condition of the country, informed us that they were going on to the large city of Nan Yang Fu that night, but would leave us two soldiers and two of their carts. Mr. Goforth did not wish them to go, for he felt it would greatly increase our danger.

Shortly after they left us, a mob began to gather outside our inn. The gate was barricaded with carts. For hours, the rioters threw stones against the gate and demanded our money. A messenger was at once sent after the engineers' party, asking them to return. We spent all that night in sleepless suspense.

Early in the morning, the messenger returned with the reply that they had failed to get help from the Nan Yang Fu official and were obliged to push on. As soon as the carters heard we had been left helpless, a panic seized them, and it was with great difficulty they could be persuaded to harness their animals. All this time, the crowd had been becoming denser, as we could see through the cracks of the gate, and they were ominously quiet. Hints had been given us of coming danger, but that was all. None spoke of what we all felt—that we were probably going to our death.

Suddenly, without the slightest warning, I was seized with an overwhelming fear of what might be awaiting us. It was not the fear of *after* death but of the probable torture before death that took such awful hold of me. I thought, *Can this be the Christian courage I have looked for?* I found a place to be alone and prayed for victory, but no help came. Just then, someone called us to a room for prayer before getting into our carts. Scarcely able to walk for trembling, and utterly ashamed that others would see my state of panic—for such it undoubtedly was—I managed to reach the bench beside which my husband stood. He withdrew from his pocket the little book *Clarke's Scripture Promises* and read the verses he first laid his eye upon. They were the following:

> *The eternal God is thy refuge, and underneath are the everlasting arms: and he shall thrust out the enemy from before thee; and shall say, Destroy them.*
> (Deuteronomy 33:27)

The God of Jacob is our refuge.　　　　(Psalm 46:7)

Thou art my help and my deliverer; make no tarrying, O my God.　　　　(Psalm 40:17)

I will strengthen thee; yea, I will help thee; yea, I will uphold thee with the right hand of my righteous-ness....For I the LORD thy God will hold thy right hand, saying unto thee, Fear not; I will help thee.
　　　　(Isaiah 41:10, 13)

If God be for us, who can be against us?
　　　　(Romans 8:31)

We may boldly say, The Lord is my helper, and I will not fear what man shall do unto me.
　　　　(Hebrews 13:6)

The effect of these words at that time was remarkable. Everyone realized that God was speaking to us. Never was there a message more directly given to mortal man from his God than that message to us. As my husband read, my whole soul seemed to be flooded with a great peace. All trace of panic vanished, and I felt God's presence was with us. Indeed, His presence was so real that it could scarcely have been more so had we seen a visible form.

After prayer, we all got in the carts and one by one passed into the densely crowded street. As we approached the city gate, we could see that the road was black with crowds await-ing us. I had just remarked to my husband on how well we were getting through the crowds when we passed through the gates. My husband turned pale as he pointed to a group of several hundred men, fully armed, awaiting us. When all the carts had passed through the gate, they hurled a shower of stones at us as they rushed forward and maimed and killed some of the animals. Mr. Goforth jumped down from the cart and cried to them, "Take everything but don't kill." His only answer was a blow. The confusion that followed was so great that it would be impossible to describe in detail each person's testimony of that mighty and merciful deliverance. But I must give the details of Mr. Goforth's experience.

Mr. Goforth's Testament of Deliverance

One rioter struck Mr. Goforth on the neck with a great sword wielded with two hands. The blow of the blunt edge of the sword left a wide mark on his neck but did no further harm. Had the sharp edge further punctured his neck, he would certainly have been beheaded!

His thick helmet was cut almost to pieces, one blow cutting through the leather lining just over his temple but not even scratching his skin!

Again, he was felled to the ground with a fearful sword slash, which punctured the bone of the skull and almost cleft it in two. As he fell, he distinctly heard a voice, saying, "Fear not, they are praying for you." Rising from this blow, he was again struck down with a club. As he fell almost unconscious to the ground, he saw a horse coming full speed toward him. When he regained consciousness, he found that the horse had tripped and fallen so near to him that its tail was almost touching him. The animal, kicking furiously, served as a barrier between him and his assailants. As he lay there dazed and not knowing what to do, a man came up to him as if to strike but instead whispered, "Leave the carts." By that time, the onlookers began to rush forward to gather the loot, but the attacking party felt that the things belonged to them, so they desisted the assault upon us in order to secure their booty.

A word as to myself and the children: several fierce men with swords jumped onto my cart. One struck at the baby, but I parried the blow with a pillow, and the little fellow received only a slight scratch on the forehead. Then they dropped their swords and began tearing at our goods in the back of the cart. Heavy boxes were dragged over us, and everything was taken. Just then, a dreadful-looking man tried to reach us from the back of the cart with his sword, missing by an inch. I thought he would come to the front and continue his attack, but he didn't.

Before that, I had seen Mr. Goforth sink to the ground covered with blood twice, and had assumed he was dead.

Just then, our son Paul, who had been in the last cart, jumped in, wild with delight at what he seemed to think was great fun, for he had just run through the thick of the fight, dodging sword thrusts from all sides, and had succeeded in reaching me without a scratch. A moment later, my husband came to the edge of the cart, scarcely able to stand, saying, "Get down quickly. We must not delay in getting away." As I got down, one man snatched away my hat, and another my shoes, but we were allowed to go.

Ruth was nowhere to be seen, and we hoped she was with the missionaries who had charge of her at the time of attack. I saw that Mr. Goforth's strength was failing fast, for he could scarcely walk, and as men began to follow, I urged him forward with the baby and the other two children. I turned to face the men and begged them to have mercy on my children, for they had begun to stone us. They stopped and listened; then the leader said, "We've killed her husband. Let her go." With that, they ran back to the carts.

I knew Mr. Goforth could not go far. We could see a small village not far ahead of us, and to this we hastened, praying as we went that the Lord would open the hearts of the people to receive us. Here again, Paul seemed to feel no fear, but said, "Mother, what does this put you in mind of? It puts me in mind of the Henty books!"

As we neared the village, men came out to drive us away, but I begged them to help us. By this time, Mr. Goforth had sunk to the ground. Putting the baby in an old woman's arms, I knelt down beside my husband. The children were crying bitterly. Mr. Goforth looked as if he were dying. The women standing around us were weeping now. This was too much for the men, who came forward, saying, "We will save you." One ran and got some stuff to put in the wounds, assuring us it would stop the flow of blood, and it did. This man helped me to dress the wounds with bandages made from garments taken from me and the children. They helped my husband, carrying him to a place to rest, and we followed them into a little hut, where they laid him on a straw bed and locked us in. We were handed hot water for bathing our bruises, food, and drink through a small window, and we could hear them planning how they would save us. We told them how anxious we were to hear news of our friends and little Ruth, so they sent a man to inquire of them.

We found that these people—the whole village—were Mohammedans and had taken no part in the attack. We felt that God had wonderfully directed our steps to that village.

All that day, Mr. Goforth lay still, but looked at times so very white that I feared the worst. Never for one moment during that day did I cease to pray for his life. And when Mr. —, one of the men in our party, arrived around four o'clock looking for us, Mr. Goforth at once got up as if perfectly well and insisted on walking to the cart. To me, knowing how he had looked that day, it seemed only a miracle. His answer to my protest was, "Only pray; the Lord will give me strength, as long as He has work for me to do."

As we were leaving, the kind villagers gathered around, insisting on my taking some old clothes to put on the children, who were almost naked, saying, "It will be chilly at night." As we went forward to join the others, Mr. — told us how, one by one, everyone had escaped. Some of us were black-and-blue for days after that incident, but besides Mr. Goforth, Dr. — was the only one seriously injured. The poor fellow had had his kneecap severed and the tendons of his right wrist badly cut, aside from many other wounds.

All that day, our friends had been waiting by the roadside, unable to proceed without carts, owing to the doctor's condition. They had joined in one petition, that God would move the carters to come. Those who know China and heathen carters will readily acknowledge that it was nothing short of a miracle—the miracle of answered prayer—that made these heathen carters come, after all they had already gone through. For come they did, five of them, which was all we needed now that our luggage was gone. We learned, too, that our faithful Chinese nurse, who had charge of Ruth, had saved the child at the risk of her own life, lying upon the child and taking many cruel blows, until greed for loot drew the men off.

We soon rejoined the rest of the party, and by six o'clock that evening, we reached the large city of Nang Yang Fu. The city wall was black with people, and as we entered the gate, the wild crowds crushed against our carts. Sometimes the animals staggered, and it seemed as if nothing could save the carts from being overturned. Every moment or two, a brick or a stone would be hurled against the carts, and that cry "Kill, kill," which can never be forgotten once heard, was shouted by perhaps hundreds of voices. Yet the Lord brought us through, and "no weapon prospered." (See Isaiah 54:17.)

When we reached the inn, a wild mob of over a thousand men filled the inn yard, and as we alighted from the cart, these men literally drove us before them into one room, which in only a few moments was packed to suffocation. For probably an hour, the crowd kept crushing us into one corner. Then those outside became impatient at not being able to get in and demanded that we be brought out.

We managed to keep some of the ladies from going out, but the rest of us men, women, and children stood facing that seething multitude until relief came in the darkness. Why did they not kill us then? Why, indeed? None but the almighty God kept that crowd back.

As soon as we had reached the city, a servant had been sent to the official demanding protection. It was dark when this man returned, in a state of great agitation. His story was that as he was waiting for an answer from the official, he overheard a conversation between two soldiers, and gathered that the official had sent a party of fifty soldiers to post alongside the road that we would have to take, with the order that every one of us must be put to death. The official was afraid to have us killed in the city, lest he should afterward be blamed. But by this plan, he could say the brigands had done the deed. So sure was this servant that we were all to be massacred that he would remain with us no longer but returned that night to Honan with the report that we were all killed.

A consultation was held to discuss whether we should we stay in the city and again demand protection or go on and trust God to open our way. The latter course was decided upon. But for a long time, the carters utterly refused to go farther with us. Again, prayer opened up our way, and by two o'clock in the morning, we all were ready to start the journey.

The official had sent a few foot soldiers to guide us to the "right road" (to the waylaying party). The night was very dark, and as we were passing through the gate of the city, we noticed what seemed to be signal lights put out and drawn in. We all felt these to be signals to the waylaying party ahead. A short distance from the city, probably about one hundred yards, our carts suddenly stopped. Someone ran up and whispered to Mr. Goforth, "Paul and Mr. — are missing." Search was made for them, but without success.

A veil must be drawn over those terrible hours of suspense. My faith seemed to fail me, and I could only cry in my agony, "If Paul is gone, can I ever trust God again?" Then I remembered how marvelously God had given me back my dear husband's life, and I just committed Paul into His hands and waited to see what He would do.

When all hope was given up of finding the missing ones, we decided to leave a cart behind with a trusted servant, and we went on. Then we saw God's wonderful plan for us. While we were searching for Paul and Mr. —, the soldiers had fallen asleep in the carts and were not aware that our carters were taking a side road until we had gotten miles from the city, far beyond the reach of our would-be murderers! We heard that the soldiers were infuriated at this discovery; but after some threatening, they left us and returned to the city. Thus, again, we saw that God was indeed *"unto us a God of deliverances"* (Psalm 68:20 RV).

Again and again that day, we were surrounded by mobs. Many times I held up the poor, dirty clothes that the Mohammedans had given us, and the story of how these had been given quieted the people perhaps more than anything.

Once the cry was raised to drag our children's nurse out of the cart, but as we cried out to God for her, the people left us alone, and we passed on. At another time, a man snatched away the remains of Mr. Goforth's helmet and tore it to pieces. I had hoped to keep it as a trophy should we ever get out safely.

At this time, we were in a pitiable condition. Most of the men's heads or arms were bandaged, and Dr. — was unable to raise his head. What we suffered in those carts, with nothing but the boards under us, cannot be told. Nine persons were packed in our cart, which under ordinary circumstances would have held only four or five. At noon, we reached a large city, where the animals could rest and feed. Then again, we saw evidence of the Lord's loving-kindness over us.

Just as we were getting down from our carts, the crowd became very threatening, and it looked to us as if our hour had indeed come. But at this critical juncture, two well-dressed young officials came through the crowd, greeting Mr. Goforth in great surprise. He had received them in our home at Chang Te Ho. A few words of explanation were spoken, and then the officials turned quickly to the crowd and told them who we were and of our work in Chang Te Ho. The attitude of the people changed instantly, and they made way for us, giving us good rooms, as well as food, which was greatly needed.

That noon, as one after another came up to us to express their sympathy at Paul's loss, I could say nothing—I was waiting to see what God would do. When Mr. Goforth told the young officials about Paul and Mr. —, they were very concerned, and they promised to send men at once to search for them. These friends in need sent with us a man of the district to guide and help us, and also wrote an urgent letter to the official of the city where we were to stay that night, asking him to give us an escort and to help us in any way he could.

At about four o'clock that afternoon, a man came running after us with the joyful news that Paul and Mr. — were safe and would reach us that night. As I listened to this news, I was overwhelmed with my unbelief and faithlessness in the hour of testing and could only bow my head and weep. Oh, the goodness and mercy of God! Never had the love of God seemed as wonderful as it was in that hour.

> Could we with ink the ocean fill,
> And were the skies of parchment made,
> Were every stalk on earth a quill,

And every man a scribe by trade;
To write the love of God above
Would drain that ocean dry;
Nor could the scroll contain the whole,
Though stretched from sky to sky.[4]

That night we reached our destination around nine o'clock, having traveled seventeen hours over those roads, with only a short break at noon. It was marvelous how Mr. Goforth was sustained, for he was obliged to start at once for the official's residence with the note I have already referred to. On the way through the street, the mob almost succeeded several times in getting him down under their feet, but God was with him, and he safely reached yamen.[5] He was courteously received by the official, who promised us protection, and sent him back to the inn with an escort.

When Paul and Mr. — arrived that night, they tried in vain to wake me, but nature had to have her way. I knew nothing until I awakened with a start at about 2 a.m. Jumping up, I started to look for Paul, and never can forget what I saw! The whole party was lying on the bare earthen floor, with very little bedding or mattresses.

I found out later that Paul and Mr. — had gotten down from their cart and had been walking behind the rest of our group. Somehow, they'd missed the road in the dark and had been separated from us. During that day, they'd found themselves repeatedly in the gravest danger.

---

4. Frederick M. Lehman, "The Love of God," 1917.
5. yamen: "the headquarters or residence of a Chinese government official or department" (*Merriam-Webster's 11th Collegiate Dictionary*).

On one occasion, when surrounded by a violent mob, one man had raised a club above Paul's head to strike him down, but Mr. — had felt impelled by some unseen power to shout, "We are not Roman Catholics but Protestants." At this, the man had lowered his club, exclaiming, "Why, these are not the bad foreign devils, but the good foreign devils, like those missionaries at Chow Chia K'eo" (China Inland Mission). The hearts of the people had seemed to turn toward them in a wonderful way. One man had given Paul one hundred *cash* (five cents) to buy some food. Another man had carried the lad on his back for miles to give his feet a rest, since they were sore. This same man, when he'd not been able to carry Paul any longer, had run ahead to try and find us. When they'd reached the inn where we had been helped by the two Chinese gentlemen, they'd found that these friends had food prepared and a wheelbarrow waiting, and also a guide ready to lead them to us!

Less than an hour from the time I awakened, we were on the road again. The official was true to his promise, and a large mounted escort accompanied us. We traveled for twenty hours that day, reaching Fancheng at midnight. Here we found the engineers' party waiting for us with hired boats, but we were obliged to remain twenty-four hours in the most loathsome inn we ever had the misfortune to be in. It was an unspeakable relief to get into the houseboats, even though we had only bare boards to lie on, and the boat people's food to eat.

It took ten days to sail downstream to Hankow. One after another person became ill. When we were still a day's trip from Hankow, a steam tug met us with provisions. Our children cried at the sight of bread and milk! We were not allowed to stay in Hankow as long as we had hoped, to get clothes and other necessaries, but were obliged to hasten on by the first steamer, which left the following morning. I was obliged to borrow garments for myself and the children from our fellow passengers.

Clothes Provided

In Shanghai, the streets were being paraded, and every preparation was being made for an attack. We learned with deep sorrow of the death of many dear friends at the hands of the Boxers. Ordered home by the first steamer, without anything left to us but the old clothes we wore at the time of the attack, how could we get ready in such a short time for the long voyage home? There was no lack of money, for our board had cabled all we needed. The question that faced us was how we would get clothes for six of us in such a short time, for the Chinese tailors were too busy to help, we had no machine to use, and there were no ready-made clothes to buy, except some for Mr. Goforth and Paul.

Again, I found that man's extremity was God's opportunity. He was true to His promise *"God shall supply all your need"* (Philippians 4:19). Even as I knelt in agony to pray, beseeching God's help, and asking definitely that someone would be sent to me to help with the sewing, two ladies appeared at the door, asking for me! These women were complete strangers, but they had seen our names among the list of recent refugees, and God had moved them to come and offer their assistance! They worked for me night and day until we had to board the steamer. Never shall I forget their Christian fellowship and practical help at that time.

But in the rush to get the older children ready, baby Wallace's clothes were neglected. There was nothing I could do but to take materials with me and make things for him on the voyage. In this connection came a most wonderful and precious evidence of God's power to answer prayer. For the first few days of the journey, I worked early and late trying to make something for the little one, who had scarcely anything to wear; but as we were nearing Yokohama, I realized I had almost reached the end of my strength. My needle refused to work; try as I would, I could not even see where to put the needle.

Folding up my work, I went down to the stateroom, and, kneeling down, I spread the work before the Lord. Too far gone to agonize in prayer, I could only quietly, almost mutely, tell the Lord how the poor child had no clothes. Rising with a great sense of the burden having been lifted, I put the work away, locking it in a trunk, then went up on deck and lay down, almost insensible from exhaustion. How much time passed I do not know, but it could not have been more than half an hour when someone came and touched me, saying, "We have dropped anchor in Yokohama Bay, and a large bundle has been thrown up on deck from the lighter for you."

"For me!" I cried. "Surely not; I know no one in Japan." Then I thought, "It is the answer!"

Going down, I found a letter from Mrs. O. E., of the China Inland Mission. She said that her little son, who was the same age as baby Wallace, had died four months before, and that the Lord had pressed her to send his complete outfit to me for my child! Opening the parcel, I found not only everything the child could possibly need for a year or more, but much more. Had someone stood beside that dear sister and told her what I most needed, she could not have done any better. Yes, surely Someone had directed her loving hands, and Someone had used her as one of His channels; for she lived near to Him and was an open channel.

Three days later, my own collapse came, but praise His great name, God was with me in the darkness and brought me through.

6

PROVING GOD'S FAITHFULNESS
1902–1908

"The safest place...is the path of duty."

O ne of the results of our gracious and merciful deliverance from the hands of the Boxers was an increased desire to make our lives tell in the service of God—to spend and be spent for Him. Our heavenly Father saw this and took us at our word, and led us out onto the path that meant absolute surrender as I had never known it before.

It is so true that "God will be no man's debtor." When He asks for and receives our all, He gives in return that which is above price—His own presence. The price we pay is not great when compared with what He gives us in return; it is our blindness and our unwillingness to yield that make it seem great.

A Hard Proposition

Many people have asked me to share the following story. Believing that it has a lesson for others, I give it, though to do so means lifting the veil on a very sacred part of my life.

After our experience with the Boxers, my husband returned to China in 1901; and, with my children, I departed for Honan, China, in the summer of 1902, leaving our two eldest children at the Chefoo schools. Mr. Goforth met me in Tientsin, and together we traveled inland by riverboat, a journey of about twenty-four days. During those long, quiet days on the riverboat, my husband shared with me a carefully thought-out plan for future mission work.

He reminded me that six missionaries from a mission station that had been destroyed by the Boxers were now permanently stationed in Changte, and that the main station, now fully equipped, no longer needed us as before. He felt that the time had come when we should give ourselves to the evangelization of the great regions north and northeast of Changte—regions that up to that time had been scarcely touched by the gospel, because of the lack of workers. His plan was that we—husband and wife, with our children—should go and live and work among the people.

To make this possible, a native compound would be rented in the center, where we would stay for a month on our first visit, then leave behind an evangelist to carry on the work; we would revisit this place, and other places so opened, as many times as possible throughout the year.

What this proposition meant to me can scarcely be understood by those unfamiliar with China and Chinese life.

Smallpox, diphtheria, scarlet fever, and other contagious diseases are chronic epidemics; and China, outside of the parts ruled by foreigners, is absolutely devoid of sanitation.

Four of our children had died. To take the three little ones then with me into such conditions and danger seemed like stepping over a precipice in the dark and expecting to be kept. But, on the other hand, I had the language and experience for just such work, the need was truly appalling, and there was no other woman to do it. In my innermost soul, I knew the call had come from God, but I would not pay the price. My one plea in refusing to enter that life was the risk it posed to the children.

Again and again, my husband reminded me that "the safest place" for myself and the children was on "the path of duty," that I could not keep them in our comfortable home in Changte, and that "God could keep them anywhere." Still, I refused. Just before reaching our station, he begged me to reconsider my decision. When I gave my final refusal, his only answer was, "I fear for the children."

The very day after reaching home, our dear Wallace was taken ill. For weeks, we fought for his life until at last the crisis passed and he began to recover. Then my husband started off alone on his first trip! He had been gone only a day or two when our precious baby Constance, who was only a year old, was taken down with the same disease that Wallace had. From the onset, there seemed little to no hope. The doctors, a nurse, and all those in our little mission circle joined in the fight for her life. I sent for her father, but he didn't arrive until she was losing consciousness. A few hours later, when we were kneeling around her bedside waiting for the end, my eyes seemed suddenly opened to what I had been doing—*I had dared to fight against almighty God.*

Made Willing in the Day of God's Power

In the moments that followed, God revealed Himself to me in such love and majesty and glory that I gave myself up to Him with unspeakable joy. Then I knew that I had been making an awful mistake, and that I could indeed safely trust my children to Him wherever He might lead. Only one thing seemed plain—that I must follow God where He would lead. I saw at last that He must come first. Before Constance's precious body was laid away, we began making preparations for our first trip.

Was God faithful to the vision He had given me? Or did He allow the children to suffer in the years that followed, when we spent months each year among the people? As I write this, eighteen years have passed since we started on that first trip, and none of our children has died. Never had we as little sickness as during that season of life. Never had we so much evidence of God's favor and blessing in a hundred ways—as may be gathered from the definite testimonies that follow.

A Testimony to God's Abundant Faithfulness

Without exception, every place in which we stayed for a month and opened as a new mission, as my husband had planned, became in time a growing church.

And I found, to my surprise, that I was able to give more time to my children and to guard them better on those trips than when in the Changte station. For in Changte, the mission compound was large, and the children were often out of my sight for hours at a time; on the other hand, the outside native compounds we lived in were so small that the children were always within my sight and reach. Even when groups of women were listening to the gospel, I was able to direct the children's lessons.

As I look back on that time, my heart is filled with overflowing gratitude to God for the wonderful grace and strength He gave for that life. My great regret is that I did not keep a record of answers to prayer. I find it most difficult to record just what "asking and getting things from God" meant at that time, but it now seems to me to have been the very foundation of that whole season of life. The instances of answers to prayer recorded here are simply the ones connected with that life that stand out most clearly in my memory of those years.

A Believing Woman Who Was
Given Exceptional Power

The first answer to prayer came the morning after our dear Constance died, and was the one that had the greatest, most far-reaching effect on our new life and work.

As I thought of facing the crowds of heathen women day by day, and what it would mean to carry on aggressive evangelism, there was one need I felt must be met—that of a Bible woman. As I prayed for direction, it came to my mind that I should ask for a woman named Mrs. Wang Hsieh-sheng.

But when I laid my request before her that she come with me, she burst into tears, saying, "I dare not. I have only one child left, and it would put her in too much risk."

Seeing how she felt, I did not urge her but told her to go and pray about it for a day, and then bring me her answer after the funeral that night. When she came that evening, her face was shining through tears as she said, "O my Shepherd Mother, I will go. If you are willing to risk your children for the sake of my sisters, how much more should I?"

Eighteen years have passed since that day. I would need to write a volume to record all that Mrs. Wang meant to me in those years; yes, and to the work itself. As the years passed, she became my beloved companion, sharing in all the responsibilities and hardships of that life, and also in its joys. I realized more and more that she was indeed a God-given coworker. Though circumstances have led me away from that life, she still remains and works for her sisters in the Changte church.

God Meeting the Home Message—"Retrench"

One of the hardest commands a missionary can get from his home board is "Retrench. My husband and I were on one of our evangelistic tours north of Changte. Every door seemed wide open before us, and the time was ripe for an especially aggressive evangelistic campaign for the heathen. But, just as we were planning for this, our station treasurer sent word that he had received a message from the home board stating that funds were low and retrenchment must be carried out along all lines.

To us, this meant dismissing helpers, and a general curtailing of our work. We faced the question squarely. Our own tithe had been long overdrawn. How, then, could we support the men we had and go on with the work that was opening so gloriously before us after years of hard pioneer preparation?

But we decided to go on as we had planned, and to trust God for the necessary funds, believing that, though the home church had disappointed us for the time being, God would not fail us.

Abundant Funds Provided

The following Friday, we received mail from home, in which was a letter from a lady in New Zealand. The writer said she had read a letter of ours in *The Life of Faith* and wished to support an evangelist under us. Her offering relieved us of the support of one man, but there were many other needs unmet.

The following Monday, when our mail was forwarded to us, we received a letter from a lady in Australia, enclosing a draft ample to meet every special need in the work for a year. She stated very plainly that she did not wish the money to be put into the general funds of the mission, but to be used by ourselves in whatever way we thought best. Indeed, had she known the special circumstances in which the letter would find us, she could scarcely have written it more exactly to fit our case.

Again, a year after this experience of God's faithfulness to meet all our needs, we needed more funds for the work. My husband, as usual, seemed quite sure that we should keep on as we had been doing and that the money needed would be sent. In spite of all the blessed lessons of the past, my faith seemed to fail me, and I spoke decidedly against using our salary for the mission, since we needed it all for us and our children's education. We were traveling homeward by cart at the time, and the matter was dropped, though I felt my husband was hurt by my lack of faith.

When we reached home that evening, a letter from a lady in Canada was awaiting my husband. He read it first, and I cannot forget the look on his face that said, "I told you so" as he handed it to me.

As near as I can recall it, it said,

My mother and I are strangers to you, never having seen or heard either you or your wife. But my mother, who is an invalid, has for some time been restless because of a conviction that has come over her that she should send you some money. So to quiet my mother, I am sending you fifty dollars.

As I read the letter, I certainly felt ashamed of my lack of faith. In writing our acknowledgment, I told them how wonderfully opportune their gift had been. A couple of months or so later, we received a reply from the son, telling us that his invalid mother passed away soon after my letter reached them, and that the story of how God had used her in this matter greatly strengthened her faith, blessing and helping her during the closing days of her life.

A Beautiful Instance of "God's Wireless"

On one occasion, when we were traveling from Wuanh-sien to Pengcheng, we reached the town of Hotsun late in the afternoon and expected to stay overnight. But on our arrival, we found that the Christian whom we had sent to arrange our accommodation had failed to get us a place, and everyone absolutely refused to take us in. While the animals were feeding and we were trying to eat our dinner of Chinese dough-strings in the midst of a curious crowd, my husband told the Christian to go out again and look for a place while we prayed.

We dared not close our eyes, lest the superstitious heathen crowd crushing against us on all sides would take fright, thinking we were mesmerizing them. So, we silently lifted up our hearts to our Father, and before many minutes had passed—indeed, before we had finished our meal—the Christian returned and greatly rejoiced, saying, "A wealthy man has offered you a fine empty place that has just been fixed up. And you can have it as long as you like, free of rent."

For three days, morning, noon, and night, we preached in that place to great crowds, and a work was begun that has continued ever since.

Life Made Easier

There were times when my faith was severely tested; and I fear too often I did not withstand the test; but oh, how patient God is with us in our human weakness. *"Like as a father pitieth his children, so the LORD pitieth"* (Psalm 103:13). The Chinese have often said to me, "Your children seem made for this life." But I know it was God's great goodness. He knew how hard the life was, and how difficult it would have been for me to continue that work had the children been peevish or hard to manage. Time and time again, we had to get the little ones up before daybreak to start on a cart journey, but I do not remember them ever crying. They would just wake up enough to get dressed and ask sleepily, "Are we going again, Mama?" Then they would go off to sleep as soon as we were settled in our carts.

A Child's Fever Restrained

On one occasion, upon arriving at a certain town, we found the place in which we were to stay unfit for the children. It was simply horrible. On either side of us, almost reaching to our door, were two great pigsties—Chinese pigsties! In front of the door were eight or ten great vessels filled with fermenting stuff that had been there all summer, and which had added to the other varied and oppressive odors. I greatly feared for the children and wanted to leave at once, but my husband seemed calmly certain of the Lord's power to keep them from all harm.

On the second evening, my youngest child became very feverish. At the time, Mr. Goforth was holding a meeting with the men, and I was almost overwhelmed with fear lest the child had diphtheria. Kneeling down beside him, I cried to the Lord as only a mother under those circumstances could pray, and at last, tired out, I fell asleep on my knees. Awakened by the entrance of my husband, I felt the child's head again, and it seemed cooler and the child quieter. The following day he was quite well. Is it much wonder that I can say I know God answers prayer?

Blessing in the Work—Converts Given

Returning from our summer holiday on the first of September 1912, we hoped to find a place rented at a certain large center where we had planned to begin work, but to our disappointment, we learned that the evangelists had secured premises in a small market village, where there was only one Christian. There was nothing to do but to go there, though it seemed almost useless, for it was the busiest season for those farming people.

On our way there, we prayed much that the Lord would prepare the people and open their hearts to the gospel. We had not been there many days when we became convinced that we had been led there, and that the Lord was opening the hearts of the people in a most unusual way. Throngs of men and women heard the preaching every day. Our evening gospel meetings, with organ and hymn scroll, were crowded—even out in to the street.

Everywhere we went, we were met with the utmost friendliness, and before our month's visit ended, we had the joy of seeing some of the leading people in the village and district come out boldly for Christ. One was the chief doctor; another was the head man in the market. In the store, through which the women had to pass to get to the evening meeting, there were three men and a young lad of fifteen, all of whom were brought to Christ. They were opium users, gamblers, and men of evil lives. Two of them are now preachers of the gospel, and one is the leader of a little growing church there.

Had I time and space, I could go on sharing cases where the same results have followed when the cross of Christ has been the pivot of all Christian teaching and prayer has been the source of power.

A God-Suggested Remedy

On one of our early visits to the city of Linchang, a woman came to me with a little child whose foot was terribly burned. Her whole foot was badly swollen, the inflammation reaching some distance up her leg. The child was feverish and seemed to be in a serious condition. On that particular trip, I had forgotten to bring the simple remedies that I was accustomed to taking with me, so I told the woman that nothing could be done. But she begged so piteously that I could not turn her away, and, lifting up my heart in prayer, I asked the Lord to guide me, if there was anything I could do.

Even while I prayed, the thought of a bread poultice came to mind. This remedy seemed almost absurd. I had never heard of such a thing being used before under similar circumstances, but I resolved to try it. Twice a day, her foot was cleansed and put in the poultice, and it was really wonderful to see how it healed. We were there for ten days, and when we left, her foot was almost completely well. The mother, father, the child herself, and, indeed, the whole family, became Christians. On a later visit, I examined the foot and found not even the sign of a scar remaining.

Not long ago, I told this incident to a medical doctor, and he said, "Why, there is no miracle in *that*! It was just up-to-date hygiene—giving nature a chance by cleanliness!"

I replied, "Doctor, to me the miracle lay not in the poultice but in God's telling me what to use; and now it is to me all the more a miracle of prayer, since you say it was up-to-date hygienic treatment."

Prevailing Prayer for Mr. Goforth

At the same place, some years later, we were conducting special tent meetings for Christians in the daytime and for the heathen at night. Just after our meetings began, the weather turned bitterly cold, with wind and sleety rain. The tent was like a drafty icehouse. My husband caught a severe cold, which became worse each day. He had a fever and severe pains in his head and chest, but would not give up his meetings. One day at noon, he came in from the meeting looking very ill, and he lay down to rest until the afternoon meeting.

I determined to confide in the Christians by telling them of my anxiety for Mr. Goforth. So, some time before the afternoon meeting, I slipped out and called them into the tent, told them of my husband's condition, and asked them to pray for him. Oh, what a wave of earnest prayer went up without a moment's pause! Tears came to my eyes as I thought, *Surely, God will answer such prayers!*

Then, fearing that my husband might arrive, I started singing a hymn. A few moments later, he walked into the tent in his old, brisk way, looking quite well. At the close of the meeting, he told me that shortly after he heard me go out, the pain in his head and chest ceased, the fever seemed to leave him, and when he started for the tent, he felt quite well. The symptoms did not return.

Women Sent to Us

On a visit to a certain out-station, after being there two whole days, scarcely any women had come to see us. We were so circumstanced that I could not leave the children. On the third day, I became so burdened in prayer that I could only shut myself up in an empty room and cry unto the Lord to send women to us, as He knew I could not leave the children. From that day, we always had plenty of visitors to keep us busy, either Christian women who were studying or heathen women who were listening to the gospel.

Opened Doors for Preaching

In Tzuchow, the first place Mr. Goforth and I had opened a station together, the people seemed much set against us. After the first period of curiosity was over, no one came to hear the gospel. As we had a nice place for the children to play with their faithful nurse—the one who saved Ruth's life in 1900—Mrs. Wang and I determined to go out each afternoon to try to reach the heathen women with the gospel. Before going out, we always prayed the Lord to open a door for us to preach. And now as I recall that time, never once did we return home without being invited into some home to preach, or at least being asked to sit on a doorstep and tell of the Savior from sin.

Supplying Abundant Workers

One of the most outstanding evidences of God's favor and blessing at this time was seen in the way He provided my husband with native helpers. To carry on the plan of work we had adopted required a good team of trusty evangelists. Time and time again, we looked to the Lord to send men and women to help us, and the supply always came.

As my husband always seemed to have plenty of men to help him, he was frequently asked by his fellow missionaries of both our own and other missions for evangelists. At first, I was opposed to his giving away his best men, but he would answer, "The Lord has been good to me; should I be less generous with my brethren?" And it certainly was remarkable how, whenever he gave a really valuable evangelist to one of our brothers, another man, even better, was raised up shortly after. The secret of his getting men may be seen best through his own words, taken from a letter he had written to a friend in Canada around that time:

We came to this little market town in September of last year. My wife had two women workers. I had Mr. Tung, the old evangelist, and a young high school graduate without experience, and the only Christian man in the district, very ignorant but with this to recommend him, that he was converted or quickened by the Holy Spirit in the Changte revival, and was intensely in earnest. We were here for only about twenty days when dozens began to inquire of our evangelists, among whom were robbers, opium addicts, and gamblers. The work went on all day and well on till midnight. We were all tiring out. We did not have enough workers. This very heavy burden forced me to my knees. I told the Lord that He was the Lord of the harvest, and that He must send more harvesters. There was a time of intense looking to God, almost amounting to agony, and then the burden lifted, and I knew that God had answered. I told my wife that I was sure that God was going to send me workers.

Now what is the result? Since then, He has sent me two Chinese B.A.'s, both excellent speakers. He moved an excellent elder to give up his business, and he has been appointed an evangelist. At this center, a scholar who was an opium user and a gambler was converted last year. His progress has been most remarkable, and it looks as if he is going to make one of the first-rate preachers. Also, two brothers here, who were among the first converts last year, help to preach, and their father—also a convert of last year—provides their food.

Kept from Smallpox

Another gracious evidence of God's overruling providence was seen in the way we, especially our children, were kept from contracting contagious diseases. The Chinese carry their children everywhere in their arms, even when sick with all sorts of contagious diseases.

I give the following instance to show how impossible it was to know when one will run into danger. Going to a certain village for a day's preaching, I took with me little Mary, who was then three years of age. We were waited on by a Christian woman who was very kind and attentive, bringing water and food for both Mary and me. Being much taken up with preaching to the women, it did not occur to me to ask why she kept her baby's face covered, for the child was always in her arms. Just as we were leaving, I asked her. Then she uncovered the baby's face, and to my horror, I found that the child was suffering from smallpox! For weeks, I watched Mary's temperature, but nothing developed.

Through repeated instances of this kind, I came to see that Mr. Goforth was right when he said, "The safest place for yourself and the children is in the path of duty."

As I recall those years of touring life with our children, words fail me in telling of the Lord's goodness to them and to me. Though there were many hard places, these were but opportunities for special grace and help. Many times, when almost discouraged to the point of never going out again with the children, there would come evidence that the Lord was using our family life, lived among the people, to win them to Christ. Then I would take new courage and go again. Oh, it is so true that

> We may trust Him fully
> All for us to do;
> Those who trust Him wholly
> Find Him wholly true.[6]

---

6. Frances R. Havergal, "Like a River Glorious," 1876.

7

THE STORY OF ONE FURLOUGH
1908–1910

*"Call upon me in the day of trouble: I will deliver thee,
and thou shalt glorify me."*
—Psalm 50:15

In the summer of 1908, I was obliged to return to Canada with our five children, leaving Mr. Goforth in China for the revival work.

Reaching Toronto, I learned that my eldest son was at death's door from repeated attacks of rheumatic fever. He was then almost a day's journey away. On my way there, as I recalled the times in which he had been given back to us from the very gates of death, my faith was strengthened to believe for his recovery again. But, as I prayed, it became very clear that the answer to my petition depended on myself; in other words, that I must yield myself and my will to God.

I had been planning to take no meetings during that furlough but to devote myself wholly to my children. I confessed the sin of planning my own life and covenanted with the Lord that if He would raise up my son for His service, I would take meetings, or do anything, as He opened the way for the care of the children.

Six Difficult Doors Opened

There were six difficult doors, however, that would have to be opened—not one, but all—before I could possibly go out and speak for Christ and China, as God seemed to be asking of me. First, the Lord would need to restore my son to complete health, as I could never feel justified in leaving a sick child. Second, He would need to restore my own health, for I had been ordered to the hospital for an operation. Third, He would need to keep all the other children well. Fourth, a servant must be sent to take care of the house—even though my income was so small that a servant seemed out of the question, and only the strictest economy was making both ends meet. Fifth, a Christian lady would need to be willing to take care of the children and act as housekeeper in my absence from home. Sixth, sufficient money would need to be sent to meet the extra expenses incurred by my leaving home.

Yet, as I laid these difficulties before the Lord, I received the definite assurance that He would open the way.

My son was brought back to Toronto on a stretcher with instructions from the doctor not to raise his head; but on arrival, he would not obey orders, declaring that he was so well he could not and would not remain still. Fearing the consequences of his disobedience, I telephoned the doctor to come at once. When he arrived, he gave the lad a thorough examination and then said, "Well, I cannot make him out. All I can say is let him do as he pleases."

Within a month, the boy returned to high school, apparently quite well. Some months later, he applied for a position as forester under the government. He had to pass an examination of the official doctor. My son told him of his recent illness, and of what the doctor had said concerning his heart, but this physician replied, "In spite of all you have told me, I can discover nothing whatever the matter with you, and will therefore give you a clear bill of health."

As for me, I did not go to the hospital, for all the symptoms that seemed to require an operation had left me, and I became perfectly well. A sympathetic servant was sent to me to do the Lord's work, and a married niece, living near, offered to stay in my home whenever I needed to be absent.

And so there remained but one unfulfilled condition—money. But I believed this would come as I went forward, and it did. Each month that followed, as I made up my accounts, I found that my receipts sufficiently exceeded my expenditures, enabling me to spend money for work in China, and to purchase things I needed for China, such as an organ. All these accounts were laid before our beloved mission board secretary, who approved them.

Trusting for Everything

Under these circumstances, I dared not refuse invitations to speak. Yet my faith was so weak that for months I never left home for a few days without dreading lest something should happen to the children during my absence. I even accepted meetings with the proviso that if the children needed me, I must fail to keep my appointment. But as the days and weeks and months passed, and all went well, I learned to trust.

> "Lie still," "be strong," today;
> But, Lord, tomorrow?
> What of tomorrow, Lord?
> Shall there be rest from toil,
> Be truce from sorrow...?
> *Did I not die for thee?*
> *Did I not live for thee?*
> *Leave Me tomorrow.*[7]

In giving the following, I wish to make clear that, had I been living a life of ease or self-indulgence, I could not have been justified in expecting God to undertake for me in such matters as are here recorded. It must be remembered that I had stepped out into a life that meant *trusting for everything.*

Apples Sent in Abundance

Before leaving China for Canada, my husband said to me, "Do not stint the children with apples; give them all they want." But when I began housekeeping, I found this was not very easy to do. Apples were expensive, and the appetites of my six children for them seemed insatiable. However, I began by buying a few small baskets, and then I did not need to buy more, for apples came in a most wonderful way. First in baskets, then, as the season advanced, in barrels. These came from many different sources, and in some cases long distances, express paid to the door. On one occasion, a barrel

7. Christina Rossetti, "Dost Thou Not Care?"

of large, hard greenings came just as we had finished a barrel. The children complained that they were too hard to eat and begged me to buy them some "snows"—very expensive apples but delicious for eating. I had purchased only one small basket of "snows" when a large supply, almost a barrelful, came from a distant friend.

Surprised by a Valentine

I feel that the Lord saw that I had given up all for Him and so showed me how He could provide, thus evidencing His love and care for my dear children.

At the end of the fruit season, we had to set up house-keeping, so I had not been able to can fruit for winter use. However, that winter, again and again, gifts of canned fruit came to us, sometimes from unknown sources. Altogether, seventy jars of the finest fruit were sent to us. I will give the details of just one of these gifts.

Shortly before leaving home for ten days, the servant informed me that the canned fruit was finished. Accordingly, I went down and ordered enough dried fruit to last till I should return. On returning home after the trip, I was greeted at the door by the children, who were trying at once to tell me that a lovely valentine had just arrived. Leading me back to the kitchen, they showed me the table covered with twenty jars of the most delicious-looking fruit and a large can of maple syrup. On a card accompanying the gift was written: "A valentine for our dear 'substitute in China,' from her sisters in Renfrew."

A Telephone Supplied

Early in the winter, it became evident that a telephone was a necessity, with my numerous calls and engagements. I hesitated about making this purchase, not being quite sure that it was right to use the money given to me in that way. At last, I prayed that the Lord would show me His will in the matter, whether or not it was right for me to get it, by sending me half the amount needed for the telephone within a certain time. Before the time expired, the money had come, so I got the telephone.

The Gift of a Fur Coat

As the weather became cold, I began to suffer on the long drives in the country to appointments and was soon longing for a fur coat. I consulted our mission secretary as to whether, if sufficient money were given me, I could put it toward a fur coat. The answer was a decided yes. There was no doubt that the coat was a necessity in the Lord's work. So I began to pray for the Lord to send the money quickly, for the cold was severe. In less than two weeks, I received the money I needed and of course bought a coat.

God's Wonderful Keeping Power

The ladies of the Winnipeg Presbyterial had arranged a series of meetings for me, about ten in all, in Winnipeg, Brandon, and other places in that vicinity. The collections in the meetings were used to defray my traveling expenses, which would amount to over one hundred dollars. On my way by train from Toronto to Winnipeg, I caught a severe cold, which settled in my throat and chest. I did not want the women to be disappointed, and also put to all the expense, if I failed them. Just before reaching Winnipeg, I was enabled to commit myself definitely into the Lord's hands, for strength and voice for the meetings. The days that followed can never be forgotten, for the bodily weakness, fever, and throat trouble were removed only while I was giving my addresses. In each case, though so hoarse before and after speaking that I was scarcely able to make myself heard above a whisper, my voice cleared for the address.

For example, while at Dr. and Mrs. C. W. Gordon's home the Sunday I was to speak in Winnipeg, I was advertised to speak that night in Dr. Gordon's church. At the supper table, I asked Dr. Gordon if he would be ready to speak should I fail. Just before my time came to speak, I slipped up on to the platform behind Dr. Gordon, who was praying, and oh, how I cried to the Lord for help and courage! The church was packed, and even the Sunday school room partitions were opened to accommodate the crowd. My throat was as if in a vise, and I felt weak and ill.

But, as Dr. Gordon introduced me, I stepped forward and was possessed by a feeling of wonderful calm and absolute confidence. It seemed as if I could just *feel* One like unto the Son of Man beside me, and never had I felt so completely and only a channel. For more than an hour, I spoke so that everyone heard distinctly, but when I sat down, my throat tightened as before. Dr. Gordon told me later that he had a man sit in the most difficult place in which to hear, and that even he had heard every word.

So it was until the end of my appointments. On the homeward journey, I asked the Lord either to heal my throat or to provide a way for me to get a needed rest from speaking, for I had many appointments awaiting me in Ontario. A few days after reaching home, four of my children were taken down with measles. During the weeks I was in quarantine with them, my throat received the rest it needed and was quite restored.

Help for the Children's Sewing

In looking over the children's clothes at the beginning of the following summer, I found there was so much to be done, and I was fairly overwhelmed. I saw it was quite impossible to do the necessary sewing and keep my appointments, too. The question that weighed heavily upon me was, "Should I cancel the meetings for which I had given my word?" My husband urged me to buy ready-made clothes, but I knew how expensive they would be and could not bring myself to do so. I went alone and laid my burden before the Lord, praying that, if He wanted me to speak further for China, He would show His will by sending me some gift that would enable me to buy ready-made clothes for the children.

A few days later, I was speaking at a Presbyterian gathering in western Ontario. At the close of the evening meeting, an old gentleman put some money in my hands. I asked him what he wished me to use it for, and he replied, "For your children. Use it in a way that will help you to be free for God's work." My heart rose in thanksgiving, and I decided to accept it as the token I had asked of the Lord. On my return to

Toronto, I spent this gift on clothes for the children, to save my time and strength for the Lord's work.

Another Case of "God's Wireless"

When busy in my home one day, the thought of two dear friends of the China Inland Mission kept coming constantly to mind, and I began to wonder if I should send them some money. Looking in my purse, I found that I had only fifty cents on hand. I put the matter out of my mind, with the thought that if the Lord wanted me to send them anything, He would provide a way. The afternoon mail brought a letter from a distant place in Ontario where, a year before, I had visited and spoken for a friend. The letter was from the treasurer of the Christian Endeavor Society for which I had spoken. He enclosed five dollars and said the money should have been given to me at the time I spoke for them but had been overlooked.

My first thought was to return it, as it would be dishonoring my friend to accept money for such a service, but then I remembered my friends for whom I wanted money, and I decided to send the five dollars to them. My husband, who returned the following morning, handed me another five to put with it, and the ten dollars was sent off.

In due course, a reply came from my friends, saying that the very morning my letter arrived, they both had been given assurance that a certain sum would come, for which they had been praying. This was to meet a need that they did not wish to bring before their board. My letter brought the ten dollars, and another letter in the afternoon mail contained a sum which, in addition to mine, exactly equaled the amount they had been asking the Lord for.

> Say not my soul, "From whence
> Can God relieve my care?"
> Remember that Omnipotence
> Hath servants everywhere.[8]

A Timely Offer

On one occasion when I was about to leave home on a ten days' trip to Montreal and other places, word came that the children's Sunday school treat was to take place during my absence.

Little Mary had no "best" dress for the occasion. I had planned to make her a white woolen dress, but now there was no time, and I knew I could not make it while I was away, with so many meetings ahead. But, that very day, a lady from our church called and said that for a long time she had wanted to help me, and asked if she could do any sewing for me. With dim eyes and a grateful heart, I accepted her offer. On my return, Mary told me of her wearing a pretty white cloth dress for the Sunday school treat.

A Daughter's Guardian Provided

Once more, we planned to leave Canada for China, but a serious problem faced us. Our eldest son could be left to face the world alone, but not our daughter of sixteen. It was necessary that a suitable guardian be found for her. I called on three different ones whom I thought would feel some responsibility

8. J. J. Lynch, "Say Not, My Soul."

toward the missionaries' daughter, but all three declined to accept the responsibility. I then saw that it was not for me to try to open doors, but that I must look to the Lord for this also. I prayed that, if He wished me to return to China, He would send me someone to whom I could commit her.

A short time passed. Then a lady whose life had been devoted to the training of young women called. Her beautiful Christian character made her the one above all others in whose care I would gladly leave my daughter. This lady told me that in her early years, she had hoped to give her life for service in China, but the way had been closed. She now felt that the Lord had laid it upon her heart to offer to take charge of my child. Years have passed since then, and she has fulfilled my highest expectations of her. Rarely has a more definite answer come from a loving Father, or one that brought greater relief and help; for this offer, coming as it did in answer to my prayers, seemed to be unmistakable proof that the Lord would keep my child as I gave her up.

The Gift of a Red-Cloth Ulster

The time had almost arrived for beginning the last preparations for the long journey to China, when one day Ruth came in from her play with her heavy coat almost in shreds, in some way having torn it on a barbed-wire fence. The coat was the only heavy one she had, and I had planned to make it do for the ocean voyage, intending to get a new one in England. I tried to find a new one in the stores, but the season was past, and I could not. Since I had no time to make another, I took the need to the Lord and left it there, believing that in some way He would provide. A few days later, a friend tele-

phoned me that her mother had recently returned from a visit
to Chicago and wished me to come over to see a parcel she
had brought for me. Oh, the relief that came when I found
that the parcel contained, among other things, a handsome
red-cloth ulster, which fit Ruth perfectly. This fresh evidence
of the Lord's overshadowing care touched me deeply. Those
who have never known such tokens of the Lord's loving care
in the little things of life can scarcely understand the blessed-
ness that such experiences bring.

> Whether it be so heavy,
> That dear ones could not bear
> To know the bitter burden
> They could not come and share:
> Whether it be so tiny,
> That others cannot see
> Why it should be a trouble,
> And seem so real to me;
> Either and both, I lay them
> Down at the Master's feet,
> And find them alone with Jesus,
> Mysteriously sweet.[9]

Too Many Blessings to Record

As I attempt to recall the answers to prayer on this furlough, so many come to mind that it is impossible to record
them all. I received help in keeping my appointments, courage and power for public speaking, physical strength, and
guidance in facing many difficult problems.

9. Frances R. Havergal, "Nobody Knows but Jesus."

It was at this time I formed a habit of getting a message for a meeting on my knees. It often seemed to me very wonderful how, as in a flash, sometimes an outline for a talk on China would come. Never having kept notes, nor even outlines of addresses, I have frequently been placed in circumstances when I have felt utterly dependant on the Lord. And I can testify that He never failed to give the needed help and the realized divine power. Yet sad it is that often at such times, no sooner would the address be ended than the Satan-whispered thought would come, "I have done well today."

Oh, is not the goodness and forbearance of our God wonderful; wonderful that He ever again would deign to give help when asked for it?

A short time ago, I asked a dear friend whose writings have reached and inspired multitudes throughout the Christian world, "How did you do it?"

Softly, with deep reverence in look and tone, she replied, "It has been done all in and through prayer!"

With deepest gratitude and praise to our ever faithful God, I, too, can testify that any little service I have been able to do has been done by His grace in answer to prayer.

> I stood amazed and whispered, "Can it be
> That He hath granted all the boon I sought?
> How wonderful that He for me hath wrought!
> How wonderful that He hath answered me!"
> O faithless heart! He said that He would hear
> And answer thy poor prayer; and He hath heard
> And proved His promise! Wherefore didst thou fear?

Why marvel that thy Lord has kept His word?
More wonderful if He should fail to bless
Expectant faith and prayer with good success!

8

OUR GOD OF THE IMPOSSIBLE

"Behold, I am the LORD...
*is there **any thing** too hard for **me**?"*
—Jeremiah 32:27

The margin of the King James Version translates Jeremiah 32:17, "Ah Lord GOD...there is **nothing** too wonderful for thee." The following illustration of the truth "What is impossible with man is possible with God" and "there is nothing too wonderful for Him" occurred while we were attending the Keswick Convention in England in 1910.

The Blessed Incident at Keswick

One evening, my husband returned from an evening meeting, which I had not attended, and told me of a woman who had come to him in great distress. She had been an earnest Christian worker, but love for light, trashy fiction had so grown upon her as to work havoc in her Christian life. She had come to Keswick three years in succession, hoping to be freed, but had failed.

My whole soul went out to the poor woman; I longed to help her. But Mr. Goforth did not know her name, and the tent had been so dark he could not recognize her again. Besides, there were about four thousand people attending the convention. That night, I lay awake asking the Lord to bring us together if He knew I could help her, for I, too, at one time had been almost wrecked on the same rock.

Three evenings later, the tent was so crowded that I had difficulty finding a seat. Just as the meeting was about to begin, I noticed a woman change her seat twice, rise a third time, and then come to where I was, asking me to make room for her. I crowded the others in the seat and made room for her—I fear not too graciously. While Mr. F. B. Meyer was speaking, I noticed she was in great distress, her tears falling fast. I laid my hand on hers, and she grasped it convulsively. At the close of the meeting, I asked, "Can I help you?"

"Oh, no," she replied, "there is no hope for me. It is those cursed novels that have been my ruin."

I looked at her in amazement and almost gasped. "Are you the one who spoke to Mr. Goforth Saturday night?"

"Yes, but who are you?"

Scarcely able to speak for emotion, I told her who I was and also of my prayer. For the next few moments, we could only weep together. Then the Lord used me to lead the poor crushed and broken soul back to Himself. As we parted a few days later, her face was beaming with the joy of the Lord.

Given a Verse of a Hymn

While addressing a gathering of Christians in Glasgow, I was sharing a certain incident, the point of which depended upon a verse of a certain hymn. When the time came to quote the verse, it had utterly slipped my memory. In some confusion, I turned to the leader, hoping that he could help me out, but he said he had no idea what the hymn was. Turning again to the people, I had to confess that my memory had failed me, and, feeling embarrassed, I closed my message somewhat hurriedly.

Sitting down, I lifted my heart in a cry to the Lord to lead me to the verse I wanted if it was in the hymn book used there. I took up a hymn book and opened it, and the very first lines my eyes fell on were those of the verse I wanted—the last verse of a long hymn. Rising again, I told the people of my prayer and the answer, then gave them the verse. The solemn stillness that prevailed indicated that a deep impression had been made. Some two years after, a newly arrived missionary in China told me he had been present at that meeting, and how this little incident had been a great blessing to him.

They cried unto thee, and were delivered: they trusted in thee, and were not confounded.　　　　(Psalm 22:5)

Provided with a Governess

Before leaving Canada, we wrote to the China Inland School in Chefoo, China, hoping to get our children admitted there; but, shortly before we left England for China, word reached us that both the boys' and girls' schools were overflowing, with long lists of waiting applicants. This was a great blow to me, for I had been looking forward to engaging once more in the aggressive outstation work.

But the children could not be left and were too old to be taken away from their studies. It seemed necessary, therefore, to find a good Christian governess who would teach the children and take charge of the home in my absence. As we traveled all the way across the Siberian route, this matter was before us. I prayed earnestly that the Lord would direct the right one to us, for I knew that to get a young woman who could fill the position we wanted her for would be very difficult in China.

We had planned to go directly to our station, but illness forced us to break the journey at Peitaiho, China, where we met a young lady, the daughter of a missionary. Many difficulties appeared in the way of her coming on with us, but one by one, these were removed; and when we continued our journey, this young woman was one of our party.

Time proved her to be truly God-given. Not only was she all and more than I could have hoped for, but the Lord answered my prayers that her young life would be consecrated to the Lord's service in China. She later was trained in England as a nurse and is now in China as a missionary of the China Inland Mission.

Rain Withheld in Answer to Prayer

The summer holidays in Peitaiho were drawing to a close. Heavy rains had fallen, making the roads to the station, a total of six miles, almost impassable. Word had come that our two children Ruth and Wallace had to leave on the Monday morning train in order to reach the steamer in Tientsin, which would to take them to Chefoo, where they would attend the China Inland Mission schools. All day Saturday and Sunday, torrents of rain continued to fall, with a fierce wind from the north.

I rose before daybreak Monday morning to find the rain still pouring in torrents. I woke the servant and sent him off to check the chair, cart, and donkeys. A little later, he returned to say that the chair had been blown over, and the chair bearers had refused to come. The carters also refused to drive, saying the roads were impassable. Even the donkey boys said they would not go.

I was truly at wit's end. I found a place to be alone, and, not even taking time to kneel down, lifted up my heart to my Father to stop the rain and make a way for the children to get to the station. I felt a sudden, strong confidence that the Lord would help, and going out again, I ordered the servant to run fast to the village nearby and get fresh donkeys. He was unwilling, saying that it was useless and that no one would venture out in the weather; but I said, "Go at once. I know they will come."

While he was gone, the children ate breakfast, boxes were closed and taken out, and the children put on their wraps. Then the rain stopped! Just then, the servant returned with several donkeys. Within five minutes, the children and their baggage were on the donkeys, and they started for the station. A few hours later, one of the donkey boys returned with a hastily written note from Ruth, saying that they had reached the station without any mishap, and quite dry; for it had not rained on the way over but had started to pour again just after they had got on the train. The rain continued for days after.

Five Pounds Sent

At the close of our four months of meetings in Great Britain in 1910, I felt a strong desire to send a gift of five dollars to five different people in Britain, to show in a practical way our sympathy with the workers in these various branches of the Lord's work.

My husband was in the midst of his accounts when I asked him to give me five pounds for this purpose. He told me it was impossible, as we barely had enough for the journey to China. As I left him, I wondered why I seemed to have the thought of sending these gifts so definitely laid upon me when there was no money. Reasoning that if the thing were really of the Lord, He could Himself give me what He wished me to send, I put the matter out from my mind.

The evening mail brought a letter from a stranger living some distance away, judging from the postmark, for the letter had no address and was not signed. The letter said, "I do not know you, nor have I met you, but the Lord seems to have laid it on my heart to send you this five-pound note as a farewell gift, to do what you think best with."

It was with a joyful heart I sent off the gifts to the five Christian workers in Britain. Had the giver said it was "for work in China," as was usually the case, I would not have used it for any other purpose.

Sewing and Prayer

How to get the sewing done for my family and yet meet the pressing calls made upon me as the wife of a pioneer missionary has been perhaps the most difficult and constant problem of my missionary life for almost thirty years. In connection with the solving of this problem, I have seen some of the most precious evidences of God's willingness to undertake in the daily details of life.

The following story must be given in detail to really be understood as one of the striking instances of how God, in His own wonderful way, can work out the seemingly impossible.

Returning home to our station from an unusually strenuous autumn touring, I planned as usual to give the month of December to the children's sewing, so as to leave January largely free for a Bible women's training class. But my health broke down, and I could scarcely make any headway with the thirty-five to forty garments that had to be made or fixed before the children returned to school in Chefoo. By the eighteenth of December, we decided to cancel the class on account of my ill health, and I sent word to all the women, except one whom I entirely forgot, not to come.

As the days passed, the burden of having hardly touched the sewing became very great. At last, I cried to the Lord to undertake for me. And how wonderfully He did! On December 28, when I was conducting the Chinese women's prayer meeting, I noticed Mrs. Lu in the audience, the very woman to whom I had forgotten to send word. She had come a long distance over rough mountainous roads with her child, so I felt very sorry for my thoughtlessness. Mrs. Lu accompanied me home, and I gave her money for a wheelbarrow on which to return the next day. I then sat down at the sewing machine. The woman stood beside me for a little and then said, "You are looking very tired, Mrs. Goforth. Let me run the machine for you."

"You!" I exclaimed, astonished. "Why, you don't know how."

"Yes, I do," she replied.

She was so insistent that at last—in fear and trembling, for I had only one needle—I ventured letting her try. It took but a few moments for her to convince me she was a real expert at the machine. When I urged her to stay and help me, she replied that, since the class was given up, she would return home in the morning.

That night I was puzzled. Why would the Lord lead this woman to me—the only one, as far as I knew, who could do the machine work—and then permit her to leave? I could only lay the whole matter before the Lord and trust Him to undertake. And, again, He answered. That night, a fierce storm came on, lasting several days and making the roads quite impassable. Mrs. Lu, finding herself unable to travel because of the storm, gladly gave all her time to me. The roads remained impassable for a whole month, during which time I did not once need to sit down at the machine.

An Incident in Tientsin

While in Tientsin with my children during the revolution in 1912, I had occasion to go into the city with my servant. We visited three stores. On our way home by tramway, I discovered I had lost a five-dollar bill and one of my gloves. I had foolishly put the bill inside the glove. Ashamed to let the Chinese servant know of my carelessness, I sent him home when we reached the end of the tram line. As soon as he was out of sight, I took the tram back to the city. On the way, I confessed to the Lord my carelessness and asked Him to keep the glove and money and to lead me to where they were. I retraced my steps to two of the stores where we had been. As I entered the second, which was a shoe store, a number of men were in the shop, but there on the floor, right in sight of all, lay my glove, and I knew, of course, the five dollars was inside. It was with a heart full of gratitude to my loving heavenly Father, and an enlarged vision of His love, that I picked up the glove and returned home that day.

More Help with Sewing

On one occasion when on furlough with several little children, and my husband in China, I had no settled home. When the time came to do the sewing for the long journey back to China, I simply had no way to get it done. I just had to look to the Lord, and, as so many times before, He was again faithful and opened the way. When shopping downtown one day, I met a minister's wife from a distant country charge, who said, "I want you to come with all your children and get your sewing done with me. A number of the ladies of our congregation sew well and will be delighted to help you."

I gratefully accepted her invitation, and while staying with her, a sewing bee was held in the church. In one week, the sewing, which would have taken me alone many weeks of hard, constant labor to accomplish, was completed.

The Gift of a Sewing Machine

The winter of our return from China after the Boxer tragedies, I keenly felt the need for a good sewing machine, as I could not possibly do the sewing for the children by hand and still have time for meetings. One day, as my husband was leaving on a deputation tour, I asked him for money for a machine. He assured me it was impossible, that we had funds sufficient only for the bare necessities. I knew well he would gladly give me the money for the machine if he had it. So I laid my need before my Father, confident that He knew it was a real need and that, according to His promise, He could and would supply it.

I was so sure that the money would somehow come that I went downtown especially to choose a suitable machine. I found it would cost thirty-six dollars. A few days later, I received a letter from a band of ladies in Mount Forest, Ontario, saying, "Please accept the enclosed to buy something you have lost as our substitute in China." Enclosed was twenty-three dollars and some odd cents. Only a day or two later, another letter came from a different part of Ontario, enclosing twelve dollars and some cents. It stated that the money was sent to help me buy a sewing machine. The two amounts together equaled exactly the sum I needed to purchase it.

It has always puzzled me how these people came to send the money in that way, for I had not spoken to anyone but my husband about wanting a machine. When Mr. Goforth returned, I was able to show him what the Lord had given me, even when he could not.

Healing for a Case of Tuberculosis

I had been holding a class for women at an outstation and staying in the home of the elder, Dr. Fan. The day before I was to return home, Mrs. Fan asked me to accompany her to visit a very sick boy whom the missionary doctor had sent home from the boys' school, Wei Hwei, because he was suffering from tuberculosis. Mrs. Fan told me the mother was in great distress and begged me to come and pray with her.

When we arrived, I found the lad in a truly pitiable condition. His mouth was swollen, his face had a ghastly hue, and a cough racked his frame. He seemed to me quite beyond hope and looked as if he would not live long.

On our way home to Mrs. Fan's, the message of James 5:14–15 kept coming persistently to my mind, as if spoken by a voice: *"Is any sick among you? let him call for the elders of the church; and let them pray over him…and the prayer of faith shall save the sick, and the Lord shall raise him up."*

I simply could not get away from those words. On reaching Dr. Fan's home, I sent for him and asked if he and the other elders would be willing to pray with me for the lad. He consented, though at first he seemed rather dubious. There were quite a number of Christians gathered around as we lifted up the boy in prayer. All knelt down, and I read the words from James. I told them plainly that I could not say it was indeed the Lord's will to heal the boy. All that was clear to me was that we must obey as far as we had light and leave the rest in God's hands, whether for life or death. Several prayed, and then we dispersed.

Early the following morning, I left for home. Circumstances prevented my return to that place, and in time, we moved to another field. More than two years later, while visiting Wei Hwei, I met Mrs. Fan, who told me that the lad had completely recovered and was then working with his father. A year after that, I met Dr. Fan again, and upon inquiring about the lad, the doctor told me he was perfectly well and was in business in Wei Hwei City.

Two Occasions of Prayer and Revival

The power of intercession is shown in the following two incidents.

In the winter of 1905, a call came for my husband to hold special meetings in Manchuria. On reaching Liaoyang for these meetings, one of the missionaries showed him a letter from Mr. Moffat, of Korea, which said, "I have a thousand Christians here who have promised to pray for Mr. Goforth, and I know their prayers will prevail with God." Can we doubt that their prayers had something to do with the marvelous revival movement that followed?

When in England in 1909, my husband was the guest of a lady in London who was noted for her power in intercession. He was telling her of the great revival movements he had been through, which took place in different provinces of China, and she asked him to look at her diary, in which were notes of times when she had been led in special intercession for Mr. Goforth. These dates exactly corresponded to the times of greatest revival power.

Fifty Dollars Sent for Friends in Need

A few months after we returned to China from a furlough, I invited a certain missionary and his wife and children to pay us a visit. Particularly touching circumstances had led me to extend this invite. Both husband and wife were in ill health and greatly needed a change. They resided in a far inland station, which was quite cut off from other missionaries. They were not connected with any society and were looking only to the Lord for their support. Just as these friends had started toward us on a five-days' journey, smallpox broke out at our station, and one of the missionaries died. A telegram was sent to them, and we hoped it would reach them before they left; but they did not receive it until they were a short distance from our station. Then the whole family had to turn around, and once more take the long, trying journey homeward. As the weather was very cold at the time, one could imagine what a terrible trial of faith the whole experience was to them.

I felt so deeply for them that I planned to send sufficient funds to cover at least the expense of the journey. But, on getting out of quarantine, I found I could not draw on our treasurer for the fifty dollars needed, as Mr. Goforth was not at home. However, the Lord had seen the need long before I felt it and had the exact amount ready. Three days after I got out of quarantine, I received a letter from Mr. Horace Goven, of the Faith Mission in Glasgow, enclosing a draft for five pounds which, at the time, was equivalent to fifty Mexican dollars. The gift came from the workers of the mission, and he stated that they wished me to accept it as a personal gift. Needless to say, the draft was sent off that same day to the needy friends at the far-off station.

Prayer for Deliverance from Temptation

On one occasion, while we were temporarily stationed at Wei Hwei, Honan, I was called to nurse a fellow missionary who had contracted black smallpox. This missionary died, and it was during the time of being shut away from everyone in quarantine that I had the following experience:

I awoke suddenly one night feeling greatly troubled for a friend in Canada. So strong was the impression that this friend needed my prayers that I felt compelled to rise and spend a long time wrestling with God on this one's behalf. Then peace came, and I again slept.

As soon as I was out of quarantine, I wrote to my friend and told of this experience, giving the date. In time the answer came, which said that—though no date could be given, as no note had been made of it—as far as could be judged, it was about the same time that I'd had the burden of prayer that my friend was passing through a time of almost overwhelming temptation. But I read in the letter, "I was brought through victoriously. I know that it was your prayers that helped me."

Led to a Lost Key

The following incident may seem trifling to some, but to me, no answer in my life ever brought more intense relief.

For this reason, I have reserved it as the final testimony of the original prayer record.

My husband had gone to a distant province to hold revival meetings, and while he was away, I went with my Bible woman to a certain outstation at the urgent request of the Christians to preach at a four-day "theatrical," which brought great crowds. The four days were enough to wear out the strongest person. For many hours daily, we had to face unruly crowds as they came and went, and at the end of our stay, I turned my face homeward, utterly worn out. My one thought was to get to Wei Hwei, our next station, where my youngest children were attending school, for a few days of rest. I knew that a sight of them would recover my energies better than anything else.

But on my way home, I in some way lost the key to the money drawer. It was Friday, and the train for Wei Hwei left on Saturday at ten o'clock. Different people came for money, but I had to put them off with some excuse. There was too much money in the drawer for me to leave with the key lying around somewhere; furthermore, I could not go without money.

As soon as I had my supper, I started searching everywhere. Drawers, pigeonholes, and shelves were all searched in vain. After hunting for two hours, and too exhausted to hunt any more, I suddenly thought, *I have never prayed about it.* I stopped right where I stood by the dining table and lifted my heart to the Lord. "O Lord, You know how much I need a rest. You know how much I long to see the children. Pity me, and lead me to the key."

Then, without wasting a step, I walked through the dining room, the hallway, and the women's guest room into Mr. Goforth's study. Then I walked over to the bookcase (which spans one side of the room), opened the door, slipped two books aside, and saw the key. So near did the Lord seem at that moment that I could almost feel His bodily presence. The magnificent part of it was not that I had remembered putting the key there but that He had led me there.

Yes, I *know* God answers prayer.

9

To His Praise

"They shall abundantly utter the memory of thy great goodness."
—Psalm 145:7

This chapter is written more than seven years after the foregoing material, in further testimony and praise to how God answers prayer.

Trusting God to Supply Needs

Returning to Canada at the time of the Great War, we came face-to-face with a serious financial crisis. We had only two options. One option was to frankly lay our affairs before the board, showing them that our salary was quite insufficient to meet our requirements with war conditions and prices. The other course was just to go forward with our plans—to get a suitable home and whatever else we required, and trust our Father to supply what was needed above our income. We decided on the latter.

One of our dear daughters felt indignant that we should have a salary insufficient for our needs, but we assured her that to trust God for what was lacking meant not begging. The day came when this child and I took possession of our new home. As we entered the dining room, we found mail from China on the table.

One letter was forwarded from the lady in Australia whose gifts, in the past, always seemed to have met some felt need. Her letter enclosed fifty pounds, with the expressed wish that thirty pounds be used for work in China but twenty pounds be used to meet some personal need. I handed the letter to my daughter, saying, "Shall we not believe that God will undertake for us? It seems to me as if our Father were beside us, saying, 'My child, take this hundred dollars as an earnest of what I am going to do for you.'"

Tears welled in my daughter's eyes as she gave the letter back, saying, "Mother, we don't trust God half enough!"

Were I to attempt to write the history of the months that followed, a long chapter would be required, but the following testimony is surely sufficient.

Prayer and Dress

It was on this same furlough that I came to have an enlarged vision of my heavenly Father's willingness to undertake in what some might term the minor details of everyday life. Missionaries, especially women missionaries, know too well how they are criticized in the matter of dress, when in the homeland and when traveling. Through the years, I have had not only many amusing but trying experiences of this sort, and I resolved to make the question of dress a definite matter of prayer. I rejoice to testify that the result of this decision became a constant source of wonder and praise. Yes, I found the Lord could guide me even in trimming my hat for His glory! That is, so that I could stand up before an audience and not bring discredit to my Master. Praise His name!

There is nothing too great for His power,
And nothing too small for His love!

My Son in the Great War

During the time of the Great War, one of my sons went to England with the first Canadian contingent. When this news reached us in China, I began to pray definitely that the Lord would use my son's gifts in the best way for his country's good, but that He would keep him from the trenches and actual warfare. My boy did not know of this prayer.

Some weeks after reaching England, he was looking forward to leaving for the trenches in France when orders came that he was needed in the orderly room, and his unit left without him. Months later, a call came for volunteers to fill the great gaps made at the time of the first use of gas. My boy resigned from his position and joined the company of volunteers to be sent to France. Just before they were to leave, headquarters sent for him and told him he was to go to the Canadian base in France as an adjutant. His duties in this capacity kept him at the forwarding base. A year later, he again planned to resign in order to get to the trenches. He began making arrangements for this step, but, when he fell from his horse, he was invalided and sent home to Canada, where he was kept until the close of the war.

It would indeed be difficult to persuade me that all this happened by chance; for one day, when I was in great distress, expecting any day a cable saying he had left for the trenches, I received a most clear assurance from the Lord that He had the boy in His keeping.

An Answered Prayer for One at Home

When I was in great trouble after our return to China, I prayed for the Lord to grant me a clear sign of His favor by giving me a certain petition for a child in the homeland. The request was a complicated one, including several definite details. A little more than a month later, a letter reached me from the one for whom I had asked the Lord's favor. She wrote joyously, telling that she had received just what I had asked for, and in just the way I had prayed.

Our God-Given Site

When my husband resigned the regular field work of Changte, Honan, it became necessary for us to find a home elsewhere. The only suitable place meeting all our requirements was in the hills of Kikungshan, South Honan. When we went there to get a site for our home, we looked for more than a week but could find no place. As we started down the hill one morning after midnight, I was keenly feeling our failure, for we had given up our old home. My husband told me later that when he had seen how poorly I'd felt, he'd begun to cry earnestly to the Lord to give us a site. And before we'd reached the station, the assurance had come that we would get a place.

A friend on the train, who was traveling third class, saw us boarding for second class and came in for a few words before getting off the train. When he heard we had failed to get a site, he said, "I know of a beautiful site that our mission is reserving for a future missionary. I'll ask them to give it to you."

A few days later, the treasurer of this mission wrote us saying that they had unanimously and gladly voted to give us the site.

I am now writing these closing words in our God-given home, built on a beautiful site—one of the loveliest spots to be found in China. So from this quiet mountain retreat, a monument of what God can give in answer to prayer, this little book of prayer testimonies is completed.

Closing Words

As I review the past and recall God's wonderful faithfulness, there has come a great sense of regret that I have not trusted God more, and asked more of Him, both for my family and for the Chinese. Yes, it is truly wonderful! But the wonder is not that God *can* answer prayer but that He *does* answer prayer, when we so imperfectly meet the conditions clearly laid out in His Word.

In recent years, I have often tested myself by these conditions, when weeks, and perhaps months, have passed without some answer to prayer, and there has come a conscious spiritual sagging. As the discerning soul can plainly see, all the conditions mentioned in the list below may be included in the word *abide*.

What the Bible Says About Prayer

Conditions of Prevailing Prayer

1. Contrite humility before God and the forsaking of sin (See 2 Chronicles 7:14.)

2. Seeking God with the whole heart (See Jeremiah 29:12–13.)

3. Faith in God (See Mark 11:23–24.)

4. Obedience (See 1 John 3:22.)

5. Dependence on the Holy Spirit (See Romans 8:26.)

6. Importunity (See Mark 7:24–30; Luke 11:5–10.)

7. Asking in accordance with God's will (See 1 John 5:14.)

8. In Christ's name (See, for example, John 14:13–14.)

9. Willingness to make amends for wrongs to others (See Matthew 5:23–24.)

Causes of Failure in Prayer

1. Sin in the heart and life (See Psalm 66:18; Isaiah 59:1–2.)

2. Persistent refusal to obey God (See Proverbs 1:24–28; Zechariah 7:11, 13.)

3. Formalism and hypocrisy (See Isaiah 1:2–15.)

4. Unwillingness to forgive others (See Mark 11:25–26.)

5. Wrong motives (See James 4:2–3.)

6. Contempt for God's law (See Amos 2:4.)

7. Lack of love and mercy (See Proverbs 21:13.)

10

Victory Found

At the close of this little volume, it seems fitting to recount again a wonderful personal experience, narrated in *The Sunday School Times* of December 7, 1918.

Childhood Yearning for the Presence of Christ

I do not remember the time when I did not have, in some degree, a love for the Lord Jesus Christ as my Savior. When not quite twelve years of age, at a revival meeting, I publicly accepted and confessed Christ as my Lord and Master.

From that time on, there grew in my heart a deep yearning to know Christ in a more real way, for He seemed so unreal, so far away and visionary. One night, when I was still quite young, I remember going out under the trees in my parents' garden and, looking up into the starlit heavens, I deeply yearned to feel Christ near me. As I knelt down there on the grass, alone with God, Job's cry became mine, *"Oh that I knew where I might find him!"* (Job 23:3). At that time, could I have borne knowing that almost forty years would pass before that yearning would be satisfied?

With the longing to know Christ, literally to "find" Him, came a passionate desire to *serve* Him. But, oh, what a terrible nature I had! Passionate, proud, self-willed—indeed, I was just full of those things that I knew were unlike Christ.

Struggle with Pride and Bad Temper

I must pass over the following years of my half-hearted conflict with my sinful self to about the fifth year of our missionary work in China. I grieve to say that the new life in a foreign land, with its trying climate, provoking servants, and altogether irritating conditions, seemed to have developed rather than subdued my natural disposition.

One day at dusk (I can never forget it), as I sat inside the house by a paper window, two Chinese Christian women sat down on the other side. They began talking about me, and I listened—wrongly, no doubt. One said, "Yes, she is a hard worker, a zealous preacher, and—yes, she nearly loves us; but, oh, what a temper she has! *If she would only live more as she preaches!*"

Then followed a full and true delineation of my life and character. So true, indeed, was it, that it crushed all sense of annoyance and left me humbled to the dust. I saw then how useless, how worse than useless, it was for me to come to China to preach Christ but not to *live* Christ. But how could I live Christ? I knew some people (including my dear husband) who had a peace and a power—yes, something I could not define, which I did not have—and I often longed to know their secret.

Was it possible with a nature such as mine to ever become patient and gentle?

Was it possible that I could ever really stop worrying?

Could I, in a word, ever hope to live Christ as well as preach Him?

I knew I loved Christ, and again and again, I proved my willingness to give up all for His sake. But I knew, too, that one hot flash of temper with the Chinese or with the children in front of the Chinese would largely undo weeks or perhaps months of self-sacrificing service.

Heights and Depths of Spiritual Experience

The years that followed often led through the furnace. The Lord knew that nothing but fire could destroy the dross and subdue my stubborn will. Those years may be summed up in a few words: fighting (not finding), following, keeping, struggling, and, yes, failing! Sometimes I was in the depths of despair over these failures; then I would go on, determined to do my best—and what a poor best that was!

Lifelong Prayer for the Fullness of the Spirit

In the year of 1905 and the years that followed, as I witnessed the wonderful way the Lord was leading my husband and saw the Holy Spirit's power in his life and message, I came to seek very definitely for the fullness of the Holy Spirit. It was a time of deep heart-searching. The heinousness of my sin was revealed as never before. Many, many things had to be set right toward man and God. I learned then what "paying the price" meant. Those were times of wonderful mountaintop experiences, and I came to honor the Holy Spirit and seek His power for overcoming sin in a new way. But Christ still remained, as He had before, distant, afar off, and I longed increasingly to find and to know Him. Although I had much more power over besetting sins, there were times of great darkness and defeat.

The Conference at Niagara-on-the-Lake

It was during one of these latter times that we were forced to return to Canada in June of 1916. My husband's health prevented him from public speaking, and it seemed that this duty for us both was to fall on me. But I dreaded facing the home church without some spiritual uplifting—a fresh vision for myself. The Lord saw my heart's hunger, and in His own glorious way, He literally fulfilled the promise *"He satisfieth the longing soul, and filleth the hungry soul with goodness"* (Psalm 107:9).

A spiritual conference was to be held in late June at Niagara-on-the-Lake, Ontario, and to this I was led. One day, I went to the meeting rather against my inclination, for it was so lovely under the trees by the beautiful lake. The speaker was a stranger to me, but from the onset, his message gripped me. Victory over sin! Why, this was what I had fought for, had hungered for, all my life! Was it possible?

The speaker went on to describe very simply an ordinary Christian life experience—sometimes on the mountaintop, with visions of God; then would come the sagging and dimming of vision, along with coldness, discouragement, and perhaps definite disobedience; then perhaps a sorrow, or even some special mercy, would bring the wanderer back to his or her Lord.

The speaker asked for all the people who felt this to be a picture of their experience to raise their hands. I was sitting in the front seat, and only shame kept me from raising my hand at once. But I did so want to get all God had for me, and I determined to be true. After a struggle, I raised my hand. Wondering if there were others like me, I ventured to glance back and saw many hands were raised, though the audience was composed almost entirely of Christian workers, ministers, and missionaries.

The leader then went on to say that the life he had described was not the life God planned or wished for His children. He described the higher life of peace, rest in the Lord, of power and freedom from struggle, worry, and care. As I listened, I could scarcely believe it was true, yet my whole soul was moved, and it was with great difficulty I controlled my emotion. I saw then, though dimly, that I was nearing the goal for which I had been aiming all my life.

Walking into a Victorious Life

Early the next morning, soon after daybreak, I knelt on my knees and went over carefully and prayerfully all the passages on the little yellow leaflet on the victorious life that the speaker had distributed. What a comfort and strength it was to see how clear God's Word was that victory, not defeat, was His will for His children, and to see what wonderful provision He had made! Later, during the days that followed, clearer light came. I did what I was asked to do—I quietly but definitely accepted Christ as my Savior from the *power* of sin as I had so long before accepted Him as my Savior from the *penalty* of sin. And on this I rested.

I left Niagara, however, realizing there was something I still had not yet received. I felt much as the blind man must have felt when he said, "*I see men as trees, walking*" (Mark 8:24). I had begun to see light but only dimly.

The day after reaching home, I picked up a little booklet, "The Life That Wins" by Watchman Nee, which I had not read before, and, going to my son's bedside, I told him it was the personal testimony of one whom God had used to bring great blessing into my life. I then read it aloud until I came to the words, "At last I realized that Jesus Christ was actually and literally within me." I stopped, amazed. The sun suddenly seemed to come from under a cloud and flood my whole soul with light. How blind I'd been! I saw at last the secret of victory—it was simply Jesus Christ Himself—His own life lived out in the believer. But the thought of victory was, for the moment, lost sight of in the inexpressible joy of realizing *Christ's indwelling presence!* Like a tired, worn-out wanderer finding home at last, I just *rested* in Him—rested in His love, in Himself. And, oh, the peace and joy that came flooding my life! A restfulness and quietness of spirit I never thought could be mine took possession of me so naturally. Literally, a new life began for me, or, rather, in me. It was just "the life that is Christ."

The first step I took in this new life was to stand on God's own Word, not merely on man's teaching or even on personal experience. And as I especially studied the truth of Christ's indwelling, victory over sin, and God's bountiful provision, the Word was fairly illumined with new light.

The years that have passed have been years of blessed fellowship with Christ, full of joy in His service. Not long ago, a friend asked me if I could give in a sentence the after result in my life of what I said had come to me in 1916, and I replied, "Yes, it can all be summed up in one word, *resting*."

Some have asked, "But have you never sinned?" Yes, I grieve to say I have. Sin is the one thing I abhor, for it is the one thing that can, if unrepented of, separate us, not from Christ, but from the consciousness of His presence. But I have learned that there is instantaneous forgiveness and restoration *always* to be had; that there need be no times of despair.

One of the blessed results of this life is not only the consciousness of Christ's presence but the reality of His presence as manifested in definite results when, in the daily details of life, matters are left with Him and He has undertaken.

My own thought of Him is beautifully expressed in Spurgeon's words:

What the hand is to the lute,
What the breath is to the flute,
What the fragrance is to the smell,
What the spring is to the well,
What the flower is to the bee,
That is what Jesus is to me!
What's the mother to the child,
What the guide in pathless wild,
What is oil to troubled wave,
What is ransom to the slave,
What is water to the sea,
That is what Jesus Christ to me!

The special Bible study that I made at that time was embodied in a leaflet. Proving helpful to others, I include it here.

Bible Study on the Life of Victory in Christ

God's Presence

The secret of victory is simply Christ Himself in the heart of the believer. This truth, of Christ's indwelling, is, and always has been, a *mystery*:

+ Romans 16:25
+ Ephesians 3:9, 5:30, 32 (RV)
+ Colossians 1:26–27; 4:3

Christ Himself taught this truth:

+ John 14:20, 23; 15:1–7; 17:21–23
+ Matthew 28:20
+ Mark 16:20
+ Revelation 3:20

It was a vital reality to the apostle Paul:

+ Romans 8:10
+ 1 Corinthians 6:15; 12:27 (RV)
+ 2 Corinthians 5:17; 13:5
+ Galatians 2:20; 3:27; 4:19
+ Ephesians 3:17
+ Philippians 1:21

- 1 Thessalonians 5:10

- Hebrews 3:6

The words "in Christ," which recur in many other passages, will have a new literalness when read in the light of the above verses.

The apostle John had a similar concept of Christ's indwelling presence:

- 1 John 2:28–3:6, 24; 4:4, 12–13, 16; 5:20

God's Purpose

As victory is the result of Christ's life lived out in the believer, it is important that we see clearly that *victory*, and not *defeat*, is God's purpose for His children. The Scriptures are very decided upon this truth:

- Luke 1:74–75

- Romans 5:2

- Romans 6–8[10]

- 1 Corinthians 15:57

- 2 Corinthians 2:14; 10:5

- Ephesians 1:3–4

- Colossians 4:12

- 1 Thessalonians 5:23

- 2 Thessalonians 3:3 (RV)

- 2 Timothy 2:19

- Titus 2:12

10. Romans chapter 7 should be read in light of chapter 6 and 8.

+ Hebrews 7:25

+ 1 Peter 1:15

+ 2 Peter 3:14

+ 1 John 2:1; 3:6, 9

+ And many other passages

Christ came as the Savior from the *power* as well as the *penalty* of sin:

+ Matthew 1:21

+ John 8:34, 36

+ Titus 2:14

God's Provision

God knew the frailty of man, that his heart was "*desperately wicked*" (Jeremiah 17:9), that his righteousness was "*as filthy rags*" (Isaiah 64:6), that his only hope for victory over sin must come from Him. Therefore, He made kingly provision so rich, so sufficient, and so exceeding abundant that as we study it, we feel we have tapped into a mine of wealth, too deep to fathom. Here are a few suggestions of its riches:

God's *greatest* provision is the gift of a part of His own being in the Person of the Holy Spirit. The following are but some of the many things the Holy Spirit does for us, as recorded in the Word:

+ He begets us into the family of God. (See John 3:6.)

+ He seals or marks us as God's. (See Ephesians 1:13.)

+ He dwells in us. (See 1 Corinthians 3:16.)

+ He unites us to Christ. (See 1 Corinthians 12:13, 27.)

+ He changes us into the likeness of Christ. (See 2 Corinthians 3:18.)

+ He helps in prayer. (See Romans 8:26.)

+ He comforts. (See John 14:16.)

+ He guides. (See Romans 8:14.)

+ He strengthens with power. (See Ephesians 3:16.)

+ He is the source of power and fruitfulness. (See John 7:38–39.)

Some of the victorious results in our life, as Christ has His way in us, are shown in:

+ Romans 8:32, 37; 15:13

+ 2 Corinthians 2:14; 9:8, 11

+ Ephesians 1:19; 3:16, 20

+ Philippians 4:7, 13, 19

+ Colossians 1:11

+ 1 Peter 1:5

+ 2 Timothy 3:17

+ Jude 1:24

+ John 15:7

For further Scripture help, I will suggest a plan that has proved a great blessing to me. Read through the Psalms and take careful record of all the statements of what the Lord was to the writers of the Psalms. The list will surprise you. Then, on your knees, go over them one by one, with the prayer that Christ may be to you what He was to David and the others.

Use a Cruden's, or better still a Young's, concordance and look up the texts under the words *love, fullness, power, riches, grace,* and so on, grouping them into usable Bible studies. For example, take the last word, *grace;* the more one studies it, the more wonderful it becomes. Here are some of its uses in Scripture:

+ Grace for grace (See John 1:16.)

+ Sufficient grace. (See 2 Corinthians 12:9.)

+ More grace (See James 4:6.)

+ All grace (See 2 Corinthians 9:8.)

+ Abundant grace (See Romans 5:17.)

+ Exceeding abundant grace (See 1 Timothy 1:14.)

+ Exceeding riches of His grace (See Ephesians 2:7.)

But let us remember that to simply know of riches will never materially benefit us. We must make them our own. All fullness dwells in Christ. It is only as we "apprehend" (which means to take hold of or to take in) Christ through the Holy Spirit that it can be possible for these spiritual riches to become ours. The slogan of this glorious life in Christ is, "Let go and let God."

ABOUT THE AUTHOR

Rosalind Goforth (1864–1942) was born in England before moving to Montreal, Canada, with her parents at the age of three. Growing up, Rosalind intended to follow her father as an artist until she met and married Presbyterian missionary Jonathan Goforth. Together, they became the foremost missionaries to China and Manchuria in the twentieth century. They had eleven children, five of whom died as babies or young children. Rosalind died in Toronto, Canada, and is buried beside her husband.